The Story of
WORLD RELIGIONS

The Story of
WORLD RELIGIONS

by Katharine Savage

Illustrated with photographs and maps

New York   *Henry Z. Walck, Incorporated*

I dedicate this book
to my two youngest granddaughters,
Margot and Frederika

© KATHARINE SAVAGE 1966. MAPS © THE BODLEY HEAD LTD. AND HENRY Z.
WALCK, INC., NEW YORK, 1966. ISBN: 0-8098-3062-0 (HARDCOVER).
ISBN: 0-8098-3401-4 (PAPERBACK). LIBRARY OF CONGRESS CATALOG CARD
NUMBER: 66-18534. PRINTED IN THE UNITED STATES OF AMERICA.

Acknowledgments

The purpose of this book is to tell the story of the birth and growth of world religions, to fit them into their historical settings, and to outline their basic beliefs. Each religion possesses individual merit, each is convinced of the truth of its own doctrines, and I have not presumed to name any one nobler than the rest.

I have in the course of the writing sought advice from experts in the different fields to correct errors of emphasis or fact. They are all extremely busy people and I wish to express my appreciation of the help they have given me. I must make it clear, however, that they bear no responsibility for the final conclusions which must, of necessity, be my own.

First and foremost I owe a special debt of gratitude to Professor Robert Lawson Slater, lately Director of the Center for the Study of World Religions at Harvard University. He read the entire text and from his great wisdom and wide experience gave me aid of inestimable value. Also I would like to thank Professor A. J. Arberry, Professor of Arabic, Cambridge University; The Very Reverent Archimandrite Timotheos Catsiyannis, Provost of the Greek Cathedral, London; Professor A. L. Basham, Head of the Department of Oriental Civilization, Australian National University, Canberra; The Very Reverend T. Corbishley, S. J., Father Superior of the Farm Street Community, London; Canon Sydney Evans, Dean of the Divinity Department, King's College, London; Professor W. K. C. Guthrie, Laurence Professor of Ancient Philosophy, Cambridge University; Mr. T. G. H. James, Department of Egyptian Antiquities, The British Museum; Sir John Pilcher, K.C.M.G., of the Foreign Office, England; Rabbi Chaim Potok of The Jewish Publication Society, Philadelphia; Dr. J. J. Ross, Deputy Principal of Jews' College, London; W. Stanley Rycroft, Secretary for Research, Commission on Ecumenical Mission and Relations of the United Presbyterian Church; and The Venerable Sanagarakshita, Hampstead Buddhist Vihara, London. I wish to mention also the initial encouragement given me by Edward Henderson, the Right Reverend the Lord Bishop of Bath and Wells, and Mr. Joseph Bishop, Minister of the Presbyterian Church at Rye, New York.

It would have been difficult to complete such a big task without the wholehearted support of my family. I must thank especially my husband and my American daughter, Christine Stiassni, who read the whole text with critical but kindly eyes.

Once more I must praise Gillian Winger. Without her efficient work, inexhaustible patience, and unfailing enthusiasm I should never have got the manuscript into print.

Thanks are due to the following for permission to use copyright photographs in the illustration of this book:
Associated Press: p. 161; Camera Press: pp. 23, 28, 39, 50, 99, 119, 217; Egyptian State Tourist Administration: p. 171; French

Government Tourist Office: p. 199; Richard Harrington: p. 123; India Tourist Office: pp. 60, 68; International Magazine: p. 148; Japan National Tourist Association: pp. 107, 108, 113; Karsh of Ottawa: p. 145 (photograph © 1960, 1961 by Karsh of Ottawa from *This is the Holy Land* by Fulton J. Sheen, Yousuf Karsh, and H. V. Morton. Copyright © 1960, 1961 by Hawthorn Books, Inc., 70 Fifth Avenue, New York 11.); Keystone Press: pp. 10, 87, 193, 249; Hans Namuth: p. 255; National Tourist Organization of Greece: pp. 128, 130; PIX, Inc.: pp. 32, 66, 81, 176, 187, 235, 252; Realités: pp. 100, 163, 209, 267; Len Sirman Press: p. 201; USIS: pp. 220, 227, 229, 265, 270; and Wide World Photos: p. 93. The maps are by Richard Natkiel, F.R.G.S.

Katharine Savage

Contents

• 9

Primitive men peopled these mountains with gods and spirits

Introduction: The Foundations of Faith

For countless years, devout and learned men from many lands have tried to express precisely what they meant by the word "religion." Their interpretations have varied according to the age they lived in, the countries they came from, and their personal point of view. But most of them agree that first and foremost religion is a belief in superhuman power.

They also agree that religious faith, in one form or another, has provided comfort and guidance that people could not find in any other way. It seems that there has never been a time when human beings were so strong and self-sufficient that they did not need spiritual aid.

Through centuries of war and peace, triumph and disaster, freedom and servitude, ignorance and enlightenment, priests and scholars carefully inscribed the creeds of mankind; but unfortunately much of their work has been lost. In recent years, however, historians, theologians, and archaeologists have added greatly to our knowledge of the past. By skillful excavation of ancient buildings and intensive research among sacred and historic documents, they have traced the great religions back to their beginnings and uncovered evidence of early civilizations. We now know the kind of life that people lived thousands of years ago, what they believed in and why.

Primitive men were occupied with the stern struggle for survival and it must often have seemed as if the odds were against them. They found themselves surrounded by natural hazards with very little protection, and lived in constant dread of drought, deluge, blizzard, earthquake, and thunderbolt. It takes technical skill to harness water power, preserve food for a bad season, and ward off heat and cold, and primitive men did not possess it. They lived dangerously by hunting and fighting, and as they had no means of controlling the mighty forces of nature they tried to make friends with them.

All over the inhabited world people became nature worshipers, linking the sun and moon, stars and wind, oceans and rivers, mountains and forests, and the birds and beasts that lived in them, with gods and spirits. They drew pictures and made carvings of these imaginary deities and gave them personal characters. They held them in reverence and awe, and offered up gifts and sacrifices to coax them into good humor and keep them calm and happy so that they would not use their powers of destruction.

As civilization spread, the religious outlook gradually changed, but the pace of progress throughout the universe has always been uneven. A thousand years before Christ, Chinese nobles wore gold embroidered robes, while chieftains in Britain painted themselves with woad and wore the skins of animals. Similarly, some people attained a high standard of religious thought, while others clung to primitive beliefs and practices as they do today. In the tropical forests of Africa, in the steaming jungles of Latin America, on the wide Australian plains, in the Polynesian Islands of the Pacific Ocean, and in remote areas of Far Eastern countries, there are people who still follow ancient traditions which have been handed down by word of mouth from generation to generation for countless years.

In the days when men traveled by sailing ship, camel, horse, or on foot, only the most adventurous made long journeys. A range of mountains or a stretch of desert separated people for centuries, and religious beliefs filtered slowly from one tribe to another. Unconsciously merchants acted as mission aries, bartering their ideas with their wares, and victorious warriors brought their gods with them and set up new altars in foreign lands. Because the sun, the moon, the sky, and the stars were common to all people, many tribes worshiped the same gods under different names.

In regions where a community learned to cultivate the land and raise crops, life became more orderly and less perilous so that there was some time for thought. In the minds of a few exceptional men, visions of a single almighty power, working for the good of humanity, began to replace fears of the haphazard vengeance and unpredictable moods of thousands of local gods. They began to talk of justice and righteousness instead of force, and over the years people listened. Gradually the way was opened for the great religious teachers to spread their inspired messages of hope and salvation. By their words and example they promoted goodness and condemned evil.

But though every religion praised brotherly love and human kindness, barriers of hate and intolerance soon arose between them. Children of one faith were brought up to believe that their way of life and thought was the only right one, and that people who did not conform to it were ignorant and wicked. More wars have been fought, and more suffering endured, in the name of religion than any other single cause.

These dark days are slowly passing. Broad-minded leaders of the various Churches are beginning to work together instead of in opposition. They express sympathy and understanding which did not exist even fifty years ago, and people of different religions are getting to know each other better. Each year they travel more and visit foreign countries. They read books and newspapers, and see in movies and on television how people of other faiths live. They compare their ideas and ideals and find they have something in common. At the same time, statesmen of many nations are striving to banish suspicion and establish world peace.

This book is the story of people and of their religions. It is written in the firm belief of the immense value of religion in the world today, and the conviction that every faith has an important part to play in the happiness and salvation of mankind.

In the present century Communism has been born, Nationalism has increased, and other political creeds have arisen and won many followers. They are powerful forces, impossible to ignore. But because they are organizations which decree that the highest duty of every citizen is to serve a man-made state rather than a spiritual power, they are not, in these pages, included among the world's great religions.

1 · The Birth of Civilization

WHEN MEN LEARNED to write, instead of transmitting ideas and information either by word of mouth or by means of signs and drawings, they laid the foundations of civilization. Through the written word the world emerged from countless centuries of myth and folklore to a measurable age of history.

As far as we now know, the first writing was invented five or six thousand years ago in an Asian country situated just north of the Persian Gulf. This country was called Sumeria, "the land between the rivers," and it was bounded on the west by the wide waters of the Euphrates and on the east by the Tigris. Today this land lies in the country now called Iraq, and it is barren desert, one of the hottest and driest places on earth. But in 3000 B.C. it was dotted with spreading palms, the farmland was well-watered and fertile, and the people who lived there were both talented and prosperous. Sumeria lay at the eastern tip of the "Fertile Crescent," a belt of arable land which stretched from the Tigris to the Nile and nourished brilliant civilizations on the fringe of desert wastes.

It is only during the last century that archaeologists have explored this part of the desert and found, buried under sand

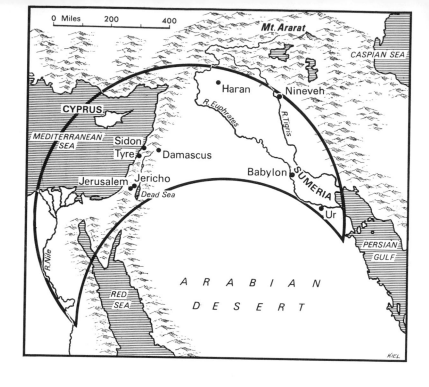

The Fertile Crescent

and clay, the city of Ur of the Chaldees, capital of Sumeria, and many other early remains. With intense excitement and infinite patience they have uncovered positive evidence of a long-lost civilization. It is a most exacting task to decipher Sumerian script, but after painstaking study scholars have pieced together the ancient records and produced a vivid picture of life in these distant days. Scripture and history agree that in about 1900 B.C. Abraham, the founder of Judaism, was born in Ur.

By this time the Sumerian people had enjoyed for more

than a thousand years a well-regulated state with a king, a carefully planned system of government, and a strict code of laws. They had a good army and were victorious in battle. They also had a highly organized pagan religion with sacrificial rites conducted by a band of priests who were all-powerful in the community.

The Sumerians were successful in agriculture, art, and trade. Throughout the country the land was irrigated by a network of canals and ditches. Farmers worked with primitive tools, but they hitched their oxen to plows very similar to those that farmers use in the Middle East today. They raised good crops of wheat and barley, grapes, olives, and dates, and carried them to market by land in donkey carts which were probably the earliest wheeled vehicles in the world, or by rivers and canals in long slim boats with pointed prows and sterns.

Sumerian craftsmen did exquisite work in gold, silver, and other metals. They fashioned headdresses for the kings and bracelets, necklaces, rings, and hairpins for their many wives. They also made jeweled daggers and elegant bowls and dishes, lifelike figures of men, women, and animals, and even children's toys on wheels.

Enterprising traders traveled far and wide bartering jewelry, cloth, pottery, and farm produce with neighboring tribes. It seems that commerce played an important part in national life, for the very first writings were concerned with business deals. Merchants used the newly discovered script to record their sales and purchases. Property owners marked the boundaries of their land with stones, minutely inscribed with the rights of possession.

Sumerian peasants and tradesmen lived in huts made of reeds and clay baked hard by the sun but richer citizens occupied fine houses with spacious rooms and shady courtyards. Most people used local materials, but the wealthy built their dwellings of stone and sent their slaves to far-off quarries to hew out building blocks and haul them back to the city.

Religion was the very core of Sumerian life. No prudent person made a decision without first consulting the gods and goddesses of the sky, sun, earth, vegetation, and above all, the moon. In this river country the gods of flood and irrigation were important powers and very influential. Sumerian kings built temples for these deities, and ornamented the interiors with glazed tiles, glistening gold inlay, deep blue lapis lazuli and other semi-precious stones. It is thought that in prehistoric times the gods and goddesses of Sumeria required human sacrifices, but that as civilization progressed, they were satisfied with the flesh of animals, fish, and birds. The priests made lists of the gifts the gods liked best: cows and sheep, goats and chickens, ducks and doves, figs and dates, cucumbers and cakes. Devout worshipers laid these choice offerings on the altars, and as a reward for their services, the priests received them in the name of the gods. The priestly guardians of the temples were also the scholars, teachers, and doctors of the Sumerian people, with a reputation for great wisdom. They not only interpreted the wishes of the gods, wove magic spells, and prophesied the future, but they taught the Sumerians how to read and write, and how to keep accounts.

As writing developed the priests became also the official historians, reporters, and scribes of the nation. Their script is known as cuneiform, from *cuneus*, the Greek word for wedge, because the priests engraved their letters with wedge-shaped instruments on tablets of moist clay. They carefully inscribed religious ritual, the laws of the land, a list of Sumerian rulers, and outstanding historical events, and it is most fortunate that they chose this method of recording their findings instead of using materials which would have rotted away with time. Once the clay hardened, it was almost indestructible and the archaeologists of the twentieth century excavated schools where the pupils had used tablets instead of textbooks and the lessons of five thousand years ago could still be learned. They also found, with jubilation and wonder, libraries where thousands of tablets remained perfectly intact.

Twelve of these tablets give a graphic description of a man and a flood which is very similar to the Old Testament story of Noah and his Ark and accounts for the layers of mud that archaeologists are probing by the banks of the Euphrates River. Many scholars who regarded Noah as a legendary figure now believe that he really lived and that the flood occurred around 4000 B.C.

Probably, when the waters subsided, the people of Sumeria moved their homes to higher ground and rebuilt their civilization. Jewish Scriptures recount how descendants of Shem, one of Noah's sons, increased until they formed a number of tribes known collectively as the Semitic people. One of these tribes, in the course of time, became the Jewish nation, which through its religious resolve and unshakable unity has had a profound influence on world history.

In the nineteenth century B.C., there was unrest in the kingdom of Sumeria and Abraham, in obedience to the commands of his own God, left Ur with his family to settle in the land of Canaan on the Mediterranean coast. Soon afterward it seems Sumeria was overcome by disaster. Fierce tribes stormed in from the east, and a writer who managed to escape described the utter defeat of the Sumerian people. It is possible that their downfall was completed by another flood, even greater than that in Noah's lifetime, and that later the stricken cities were gradually stifled by shifting sand creeping in from the desert. For nearly four thousand years they lay silent and forgotten.

But though the political power perished the learning lived on in other lands. It spread westward to Egypt and the rising empires of Assyria and Babylon, thence to Greece, and finally to the countries of Europe and the Americas. It also filtered eastward through the mountains of Persia to the banks of the Indus River. It is only in recent years that Sumeria has been recognized as the probable source of both Eastern and Western culture and civilization.

2 · The Glory That Was Egypt

THE EGYPTIANS DID NOT develop a writing as early as the Sumerians, but they were undoubtedly in contact with them and studied their customs. They may even have been related, for no one knows when the first settlers arrived on the banks of the Nile or where they came from. It is likely that wandering tribes from both West Asia and North Africa congregated on the fertile belt of land by the great river, because it was the only green strip where they could grow crops and make a living in the midst of a vast arid desert.

The age of factual history begins about 3000 B.C. when King Menes ruled over a united Egypt and gave his name to the first of many royal dynasties. The majestic palaces, temples, and tombs which remain today provide lasting evidence of the prosperity and power of Egyptian monarchs, and their devotion to numerous pagan gods.

The earliest records show that Egyptians recognized divine power in the wonders of nature and in beasts, birds, and fishes. These animal gods kept their earthly shape and character. They were either kind and helpful like the cow, the dog, and the ram, or fierce and cruel like the vulture, the crocodile, and the cobra.

The people endowed each one with a special sphere of interest. When women were having babies they brought gifts to a pregnant hippopotamus goddess called Thoeris, the Great One, trusting that she would help them to produce perfect children. There was also a frog goddess who attended births and had a devoted following. Thoth, god of wisdom and the inventor of writing, was worshiped in the guise of a baboon or a bird. Archaeologists have found too an animal with a snout like a badger, a body like a greyhound, pointed ears, and a tail standing up like a mast, which does not seem to resemble any single living beast.

Every region had its own gods, and their popularity waxed and waned according to circumstances. If the rule of one province was successful other provinces adopted his gods, but if he was a failure even his own people discarded them. From this multitude of supernatural beings there emerged over the centuries a few national figures and a host of minor gods with local connections.

As their civilization advanced the Egyptians transformed their gods and goddesses into human shape, giving them greater dignity and understanding than their animal predecessors. It is noticeable that during, and even after, the change some deities combined the features of man and beast. One of the most popular was Bes, a dwarf with a lion's head, who people believed warded off the dangers of the desert and brought happiness to many homes.

The foremost Egyptian deities were spirits of the universe and of familiar landmarks. Osiris, lord of eternity and the under-

Thoth, the Egyptian god of wisdom

world, god of crops and of the Nile, commanded widespread reverence. For untold centuries Egyptians were fascinated by the mystery and invincible strength of the great river. It was the lifeline of Egypt, providing means of transport and moisture for crops. Even the crocodiles that wallowed in its warm waters were held sacred.

Legends relate how Osiris was murdered and cut into fourteen pieces by Seth, the dreaded god of destruction, whose burning breath shriveled up men and their crops; but they end on a note of thankfulness because Isis the Great Mother, who was both sister and wife of Osiris, by her outstanding virtue reassembled his body. Later her son Horus fought Seth to avenge his father's suffering. The Egyptians adored Isis and loaded her altars with gifts. Sculptors made images of the Great Mother holding her infant son lovingly in her arms. When European Christians came to Egypt hundreds of years later they were astonished to find these statues so like those of their own Madonna and child.

Higher than all the gods and goddesses of moon and stars, storm and inundation, rocks and vegetation, stood Re, or Ra, the sun god, lord of the universe, creator of everything. He lived in the sky and was linked with Amen, god of the air, in a dual deity. Sometimes the mighty Amen-Re was represented with a man's body and a ram's head, while Mut his divine wife was originally a vulture goddess but later portrayed as a woman.

The Egyptians honored fertility, both in human beings and in the land. They liked family life and longed for lots of children and plentiful crops to feed them on. In the great city temples there were formal festivals for the fertility gods, and in every village people made their humble offerings to familiar and friendly spirits and prayed for good luck.

Egyptians of all ranks and classes set their hearts on immortality, for they had a passionate zest for living. They saw plants springing to new life each year and reckoned that by the laws of nature men must also be reborn. They pictured an ideal kingdom after death filled with the things they had enjoyed most on earth, and did everything they could to ensure that their bodies should be preserved to provide a dwelling place for Ka, the "shining spirit" which they believed existed in everyone. Ka passed from worldly life to the grave and then returned to inhabit the corpse forever. The poor could not afford the luxury of preparing for future existence, but when wealthy Egyptians died their bodies were embalmed by a long and complicated process lasting seventy days. These "mummies" looked as lifelike as the embalmers could possibly make them, and they were buried with pomp and ceremony.

Egyptian kings were held in deep reverence by their subjects who believed that they were descendants of the gods, sons of the mighty Re, and possessed of divine power. About 2650 B.C. a new dynasty came to power and a most remarkable man named Imhotep won favor at court. He was an architect, scholar, and magician. He designed the first substantial stone structures in Egypt and introduced the age of the pyramids. These gigantic piles of granite and limestone were royal tombs, modeled on prehistoric burial mounds, and the builders intended them to last through eternity. Later the kings and queens built temples to the gods and temple tombs for their own remains at Memphis, Thebes, Karnak, and other important cities. They also ordered elaborate tombs to be cut out of the living rock in the cliffs overlooking the Nile, in the Valley of the Kings near Thebes and at Aswan, higher up the Nile, and ornamented them with giant stone effigies in their own likeness.

Every succeeding monarch tried to surpass the others in magnificence, and their burial places were as grand as their palaces. As soon as they were crowned they began to build their

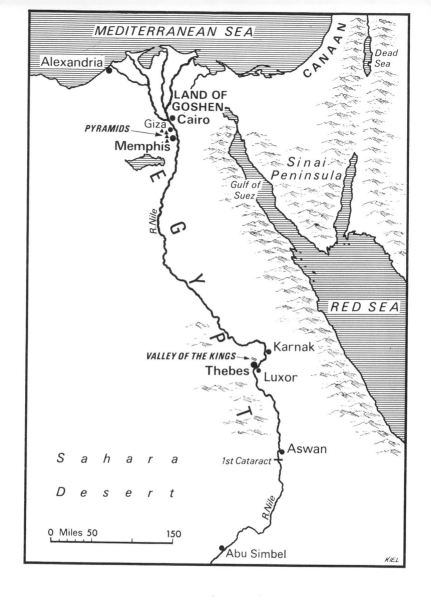

Ancient Egypt

tombs, commissioning the best sculptors and artists to decorate the walls with religious scenes, and installing fine furniture. They arranged too for exquisite pottery and glass, costly jewels, fashionable clothing, and an ample supply of food to be laid in for the after-life. The warmth and dryness of the Egyptian air miraculously preserved the contents of the tombs. Modern archaeologists who unsealed the doors were stunned to find that after thousands of years even the food was recognizable and that the cosmetics provided for the queens had not crumbled to dust.

This royal passion for building was satisfied by the labor provided partly by prisoners of war and partly by Egyptian peasants. Each year from June to October the Nile overflowed its banks and during this period of inundation farming came to a standstill. Kings and nobles conscripted the peasants and sent them to hew stone in the quarries and transport it to the construction sites. Then stonemasons and sculptors, working with flint chisels and hammers, and carpenters, using tools made mainly of bronze, set to work. It took strength and skill to transform the rough stone blocks into delicately carved wall surfaces, fluted pillars, and burnished figures of men and gods.

Every king was a high priest in his own right, a sacred link between the gods and mankind. There was a world of difference between the official state cult, or system of worship, and the humble homage of the ordinary people who put their faith in witchcraft and magic, and wove spells to protect themselves from the perils of famine and disease.

The great temples were closed to the general public. Each contained a central shrine, sacred to its special deity, and ap-

Temple of Ramses II at Abu Simbel

proached only by the king, the priests, and a very few privileged people. At festival times the images of the gods and goddesses were carried in procession through the streets, sometimes to other temples to visit particular gods, or simply as a traditional outing. On these occasions the populace paid homage as the procession passed by. Many of these festivals were timed to coincide with seasonal events such as the harvest or the inundation. In the second month of the inundation, at the feast of Opet, amidst scenes of intense excitement, a statue of the great god

Amen traveled by boat up the Nile, from Karnak to nearby Luxor for a reunion with Mut, the divine wife and mother.

Ordinary people played no part in the daily ritual of the temple. In theory the king himself visited every god in person, but as this was clearly impossible he appointed priests as deputies to take his place, except on the most important feast days. Before the ceremony could begin, the king or priest was purified with water from a sacred pool. Then he lighted a fire and burned incense as an offering to the god. After this the shrine was unsealed, the doors opened and the god removed from his usual resting place. The priest who was in attendance undressed the godly image, washed and reclothed it for the new day. A ritual feast was offered course by course, and when the shrine had been purified once more with incense the doors were sealed until the following morning. Before the priest left he carefully swept the floor before the shrine, removing every sign of human footprint.

It is difficult to understand the purpose which lay behind the strange gods and elaborate ritual of the official religion of early Egypt. But it is certain that in their private lives people had moral standards that they could be proud of. Egyptologists have translated the inscription on the tomb of Nefer-sekhem-re, a court official who lived two thousand years before Christ: "I judged the case of two partners until they were satisfied. I rescued the wretched from one who was more powerful than he. Insofar as I was able I gave bread to the hungry, clothes to the naked. I brought the stranded man to land. I buried him who had no son. I made a boat for him who had no boat. I feared my father. I was gracious to my mother." This was how he wished to be remembered.

The priesthood was a skilled and honored profession which often passed from father to son, though some laymen took on priestly duties on certain occasions. Priests lived in the temples and were by habit and tradition scrupulously clean, with shaven heads and glistening white robes.

In addition to their religious duties the priests were the educators of Egypt. They taught in the temple schools and studied mathematics, medicine, and literature. By 3000 B.C. the Egyptians had discovered how to make paper from the stems of the papyrus plant which grew in profusion on the banks of the Nile. As a system of writing developed, the priests were able to document their knowledge for future reference. They joined sheets of papyrus into long scrolls, many of which are still legible. No ancient civilization ever left a clearer account of its achievements. Astronomers invented a calendar and marked on it the festivals of the gods which were celebrated most methodically.

Egypt reached the peak of imperial power about 1500 B.C. under King Thutmose III who, by a series of victorious military campaigns, extended his domains deep into Asia. At this time the term Pharaoh came into use. It meant "great house" or "palace" and was associated with Egyptian rulers for many centuries. Every vassal state paid Thutmose tribute and the Egyptian fleet commanded the Mediterranean trade routes. The royal coffers were bulging with gold and the markets full of merchandise. This wealth was unevenly distributed among the people of Egypt, for the nobles, merchants, and priests were immensely rich and the peasants, serfs, and slaves desperately poor.

About 1375 B.C. the great-great-grandson of the mighty conqueror Thutmose came to the throne when he was still a boy. This young Pharaoh was an idealist, and he devoted his reign to reforming the religious beliefs of his countrymen. He changed his name from Amenhotep, meaning "Amen is satisfied," to Akhenaten, meaning "it pleases Aton," and tried to abolish the cult of Amen-Re from the land. In its stead he introduced the cult of Aton, a new sun-god, who he claimed was the creator of the world and all upon it, the sky and everything in it. Akhenaten composed his famous Hymn to Aton: "Thou createst the Nile in the Underworld and bringest it forth according to thy will to give life to mankind, even as thou didst create them for thyself, lord of all of them, who are weary by reason of them, lord of every land, who risest for them, Disk of the day, great of might." It was the first hymn to a single god preserved in the literature of the world. Akhenaten cared little for worldly power and neglected affairs of state to devote himself to his new faith. For a time the priests were forced to accept the royal decrees, but when Akhenaten died, he was succeeded by his son Tutankhamen, and monotheism, or the worship of one god, disappeared from Egypt and the people returned to their former well-established gods.

It is thought that by this time Semitic people, descendants of Abraham, had found their way to Egypt and settled in the Land of Goshen, near the Nile delta. They were foreign, subject to Egyptian law, and were doubtless conscripted as forced labor under hard taskmasters. In 1304 B.C., the Pharaoh Ramses II

The golden coffin of Tutankhamen

came to the throne and ruled for sixty years. It was probably during this reign that Moses, the great Jewish leader, took his people out of bondage in the Land of Goshen, far into the wilderness in search of the land that their God had promised them.

Egyptian supremacy lasted until about 1200 B.C., but from this date onward the Pharaohs never again held power in the outside world. Invading armies closed in from Libya in the west and Assyria, Babylon, and Persia in the east. Centuries of warfare slowly sapped Egyptian strength, and the Phoenicians and other "sea peoples" seized control of the Mediterranean trade routes. In the year 332 B.C., Alexander the Great set out from Greece and defeated the Persian forces which were occupying Egypt. He respected local beliefs, spared the temples, founded the city of Alexandria, and persuaded the Egyptian people to accept him as Pharaoh. After Alexander's death, Ptolemy, one of his most trusted generals, seized the Egyptian throne and founded a dynasty which lasted for almost three hundred years. But the days of Egyptian splendor were ending. Roman power spread through the Mediterranean countries, and in 30 B.C., Egypt became one of many Roman provinces.

In the course of military conquest and civil occupation, thousands of Greek and Roman citizens witnessed the wonders of Egyptian civilization. They looked with amazement at the towering pyramids, and gazed with admiration at the temples of Memphis, Thebes, Karnak, and Luxor. They were deeply impressed by the lonely grandeur of the Valley of the Kings. When they went home they described everything they had seen and people were attracted by a faith which had endured for three thousand years. Egyptian gods and goddesses were transplanted to countries where they took their places beside foreign deities, until finally they were swept aside by Jewish, Christian, and Islamic belief in one almighty God.

3 · A People of One God

ABRAHAM OF UR in the Chaldees, born in about
1900 B.C., was the patriarch of Judaism and the ancestor of the
Jewish people, deeply religious and very brave. He was not
wholly satisfied with the teaching of his forefathers and questioned the wisdom of the many gods of Sumeria. Abraham
prayed for help from a supreme God in whom he could put his
entire trust, and in the course of time an almighty power revealed
itself to him and he responded readily to the call. He hailed this
invisible and overwhelming presence as Jehovah, the great Lord
he was seeking, and swore to obey his every command.

When the Lord commanded Abraham to leave Sumeria and
take his family to the distant land of Canaan, the patriarch did
not hesitate. He set out on the long and dangerous journey
confident of divine protection for himself and his family along
the way.

It was eight hundred miles as the crow flies from Ur to
Canaan, but this direct route lay across the Syrian Desert where
there was no protection from the blinding sun, and practically no
water. The only people who inhabited this barren region were
wandering tribesmen who frequently massacred travelers and

seized their possessions. So Abraham took his little party by a much longer route, first to the town of Haran which lies in the country that is now Turkey, and then southward along the Mediterranean coast by the ancient caravan road which linked the cities of the Euphrates to those of the Nile. He must have paused at the busy trading center of Damascus and seen the heavily laden pack animals lumbering in from east and west, and merchants exchanging their goods: linen, ivory, and gold from Egypt for silver, cedar wood, and lapis lazuli. He could not settle with his family in the coastal plain among the fruitful orchards, gardens, and vineyards, because there were not enough of them to take rich land and hold it. Abraham led them on to hilly country where it was harder to grow crops but where he hoped to settle in peace. This was the part of Canaan which was later called Palestine (land of the Philistines), and is today divided between Jordan and the new state of Israel.

These strangers from across the Euphrates were called Hebrews, probably from an ancient word meaning "the other side," and the name stuck to them wherever they went. All the male Hebrews were circumcised as a religious rite, a custom which has now spread to many people of other faiths. Circumcision distinguished the descendants of Abraham from the surrounding tribes, and they took pride in being a separate people.

The records of this period of Jewish history are contained in the holy writings now revered by Jews as the Torah and by Christians as the Old Testament, the first half of their Bible. The first book is called Genesis, and it tells how the Lord appeared to Abraham and made a Covenant with him, a solemn pact promising that if Abraham obeyed his word he would become the father of many nations. And the Lord gave Abraham the land of Canaan for his people forever. This Covenant became a treasured possession of the Jewish people, and bound them together at times of desperate peril. Abraham built an altar in Canaan as a sign of thanksgiving for the love of the Lord.

Life was hard in the hills, and the Hebrews struggled to protect their wells and flocks from invading tribes. But they worked diligently in the fields, planted corn and grapes, and managed to make a living.

Isaac, son of Abraham, and Jacob, grandson of Abraham, are outstanding figures in Hebrew history. Isaac had two sons, Esau and Jacob, and the Old Testament relates how Jacob stole his elder brother's birthright and became leader of the Hebrew people. At God's command Jacob changed his name to Israel. Then Esau saw that this brother was chosen as a leader among men, and forgave him his treachery. Israel had twelve sons, each of whom founded a family under his own name. In the course of time these families grew into tribes which were known as the Children of Israel.

The elder sons of Israel were jealous of their brother Joseph because he was their father's favorite, and they sold him to an Egyptian slave dealer. He won favor in the eyes of his captors, and was awarded a post in the government, becoming Viceroy of Egypt. It is possible that when Joseph arrived in Egypt he found himself among friends. The Hyksos, a shepherd tribe from Western Asia, had invaded the Nile lands and overthrown the reigning monarch. Joseph served them wisely and well. He looked to the future and realized that though Egypt had enjoyed years of plenty, the time was bound to come when crops would fail and the people go hungry. So he built storehouses in all the cities and filled them with grain. A few years later farmers had bad harvests and famine spread through the land. Then Joseph opened up his granaries and sold corn to the Egyptians, and they were grateful for his foresight.

There was also famine in Canaan and Israel sent his sons with empty sacks to buy corn in Egypt. Joseph recognized his brothers and forgave them the wrong they had done him. He filled their sacks without payment, and encouraged them to move their flocks from the bare hills of Canaan to the fertile fields near the Nile delta, which are known as the Land of Goshen. The Children of Israel settled down happily and very little is known of them for the next two hundred years. Evidently during this period the Hyksos grew soft and lazy and lost their authority. The Egyptians rebelled against a weakening government and finally drove the Hyksos out. In the fifteenth century B.C., a new Egyptian dynasty came to power and built a great empire.

This was the age of massive monuments, each on a grander scale than the one before. Slaves toiled and died on the giant construction sites and the kings became short of labor. They saw that the Hebrew herdsmen in the Land of Goshen were strong and reliable, so they put them to work. The Children of Israel were forced to obey Egyptian masters but they still clung to their own beliefs and way of life. The pagan priests were angry because these foreigners worshiped a single god and the king and his advisers were afraid that they would grow strong enough to cause trouble in the state. So a government order went out that every Hebrew boy baby should be killed at birth. The girl babies were spared so that they could grow up, marry into Egyptian families, and learn Egyptian ways.

Some Hebrew mothers defied the cruel edict and their babies survived Egyptian persecution. Among them was Moses, who grew up to be an outstanding leader, resolute and courageous, the greatest lawgiver in history. He delivered the Children of Israel from bondage and made them into a nation. He confirmed the Covenant that the Lord had made with Abraham and gave it to his people to hold forever.

The Bible relates how, in obedience to the instructions of the Lord, Moses miraculously led the Children of Israel across the Red Sea, and how their Egyptian pursuers perished in the angry waves. Recent studies offer an explanation for the miracle, for there is a lake near the Nile delta called the Sea of Reeds where, from time to time, strong winds drive back the waters and the shallows become dry land. When the wind changes, the waters return and the passage is difficult and dangerous. This exodus from Egypt proved to the Israelites that they were truly a chosen people, safe in the protection of the Lord.

Moses did not take the main coastal road from Egypt to the Promised Land of Canaan. Instead he turned into a narrow coastal plain. The Children of Israel traveled slowly with their tents and herds. They were hemmed in by gaunt sandstone mountains on their left and the Red Sea on their right, and every day the land became more parched and the mountains more

The Wilderness

rugged. Food was scarce and wells far apart. At each one they quenched their thirst and filled their water bags before they plodded on.

Two months after they left Egypt they pitched their tents in the wilderness beneath the towering peak of Mount Sinai.

The Book of Exodus tells how Moses left his people in the dusty plain, went alone up the mountain, and remained there for forty days while he received the word of God. Amid thunder and lightning the Lord descended, hidden by the smoke of a great devouring fire. The Children of Israel watched and waited in awe, until the voice of a mighty trumpet rang out. Then God spoke to Moses and gave him Ten Commandments, writing them with his own finger on stone tablets so that they should never be forgotten. When Moses came down from the sacred mountain, he was horrified to find that the people had lost faith in God, and had begun to worship instead a golden calf which they had made. Moses was so angry he broke the tablets and put three thousand Israelites to death.

The following day, however, the Lord told Moses to cut two new tablets and he wrote once more the Ten Commandments. Moses returned triumphantly to his people, and gave them the Laws of the Lord. The first and most important was "Thou shalt have no other gods before me." The Commandments also set aside the Sabbath, the seventh day of every week, for prayer and rest; they forbade murder, theft, and dishonesty, and decreed that the Children of Israel should obey their parents and respect their neighbors. They showed the way to holiness, righteousness, and justice; and laid the foundations of the Hebrew nation in which people worshiped God and loved each other as brothers.

According to the instructions God gave Moses, these sacred tablets were reverently preserved in a wooden chest, known as the Ark, and sheltered by a tabernacle, or tent. Whenever the Children of Israel traveled, they carried the Ark with them, but they moved at the times when Moses saw that God willed it. Often a cloud covered the tabernacle and pillars of fire walled it in. Only when the Ark was clearly visible did the followers of Moses pack their tents to start for the Promised Land.

For forty years Moses led the Children of Israel forward. They had never known easy living, but the hardships of the wilderness were so great that many of them faltered. This was a savage age; death by violence was frequent and bloodshed commonplace. Moses saw no reason to show mercy to sinners. On one historic occasion, he too failed in the eyes of the Lord. The Israelites were crying out with thirst, Moses was in despair, and for a moment even he showed a lack of faith. When the Lord commanded Moses to cause water to gush from a nearby rock, he did so by striking the rock with a rod, instead of by using the words of the Lord. His punishment for doubting the Lord was severe, for the Lord decreed that he should not live to bring his people into the Promised Land. When at long last a line of green hills arose in the distance, the weary travelers could scarcely believe their eyes. In accordance with the commandment of the Lord, Moses died within sight of the Promised Land, about twelve hundred years before the birth of Christ. Before he died he proclaimed to his people: "Hear, O Israel: the Lord our God is one Lord."

The twelve tribes saw the River Jordan below them and the city of Jericho fringed with palm trees and olive groves. They went on to capture the city, but Canaanite armies drove them out of the valleys to the high stony ground above. It was not the land of milk and honey that the Israelites had hoped for, but far better than the wilderness. They changed their tents for houses, built altars (high places) to honor their God, and settled down to make a living.

Trouble in Palestine is as old as history. It is a poor country with little to offer conquering kings, but it lies at the junction of Africa and Asia, and it was fated to be a battleground between the armies of East and West. The Israelites soon saw that their only chance of survival was to unite under a single ruler. So they chose Saul as a warrior king to secure their frontiers from the invading Philistines. It was a sad blow for the new nation when Saul's armies were defeated and he killed himself in shame.

He was succeeded by King David, glorified in the scriptures as an inspired sovereign, soldier and statesman, poet and musician. He won the loyalty of all the tribes, brought peace to the land, and made Jerusalem the religious capital of a united nation. David reigned for forty years, leading his people first in war with his sword, and then in praise with his harp. The Psalms of David are an everlasting testimony to the greatness of those days. It seemed to the people of Israel that they were safe at last. They sang jubilantly, "The Lord is my light and my salvation; whom shall I fear? The Lord is the strength

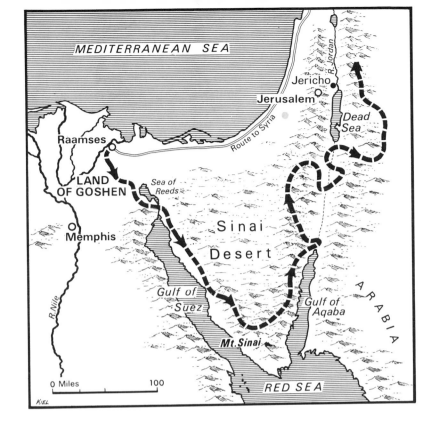

of my life; of whom shall I be afraid?"

When Solomon, son of David, came to the throne, he added prosperity to the existing peace. He was enterprising and ambitious and won a reputation for great wisdom. He opened up copper mines in the Sinai Desert, brought in technicians and shipbuilders from the neighboring country of Phoe nicia, and built a fleet of trading vessels. They sailed from Red Sea ports for distant destinations and returned, so the Bible says, laden with precious cargoes of "gold and silver, ivory, and apes, and peacocks" to enrich his court. At the same time Solomon conscripted thousands of workmen to bring stone and timber to Jerusalem for a magnificent temple which took seven years to build. When the Temple was finished he designed an even more splendid palace which took another thirteen years to complete. But the glory of Solomon's reign was all on the surface and it faded fast. He taxed his people unmercifully to pay for the upkeep of his court, and he neglected the first Commandment of the Lord. He married foreign princesses, and, despite the protests of the Hebrew priests, allowed them to set up shrines to their own pagan gods.

Once the faith of Israel was divided between Judaism and paganism, the main strength of the nation declined and the people drifted apart. Ten tribes took the northern part of Palestine, and called it Israel. They set up images of golden calves and worshiped a god named Baal. Only the tribes of Benjamin and Judah remained loyal to the House of David. They proclaimed Judea an independent state, with Jerusalem as its capital and the Lord of Abraham as its guide.

For two hundred years Israel and Judea existed as separate kingdoms, but they were surrounded by powerful nations, preparing for campaigns of conquest. In 721 B.C. an Assyrian army stood before the gates of Jerusalem. The city was miraculously saved by an epidemic which swept through the enemy ranks and forced them to withdraw. Israel had already collapsed before Assyrian might and the ten tribes lost their identity and disappeared from history forever. The tiny state of Judea stood alone to carry on the proud Hebrew tradition.

During these troubled years prophets defended their religion against the idolators of Baal and reprimanded anyone who disobeyed the Lord's Commandments. The priests officiated in the Temple, taking care of the ritual and leading the congregation in prayer. The prophets were men of the world and also servants of the Lord. They acted as the voice of God, renewing his Covenant and linking his presence to all the happenings of life. They saw divine purpose in the everyday events which linked the past to the present and the future. The prophets gave history a special meaning which has remained with the Jewish people ever since. They regard it as a heritage and a trust, a unique expression of God's everlasting plan for his Chosen People.

Elijah, the first of the great Hebrew prophets, fired by heavenly inspiration and sustained by unwavering zeal, thundered out his message against the prophets of Baal. On Mount Carmel, near Jerusalem, in the presence of a large gathering, he fought four hundred and fifty of them with accusations of false belief and threats of dire punishment, blaming them for the prevailing drought and every other current disaster. He so convinced the watching people of God's grace that they condemned the idolators to death and executed every one. The Bible relates how, at the end of his life, Elijah was swept up to heaven in a whirlwind.

His work was carried on by Elisha, an ardent disciple,

and many other prophets, foremost among them Amos, Hosea, Isaiah, Jeremiah, and Ezekiel.

They concerned themselves not only with moral standards, but also with political, social, and individual behavior. They proclaimed the need for true worship and righteousness in all things. They denounced injustice and oppression. They were passionate in their allegiance to the Lord and in their defense of the day-to-day rights of man. At times of unrest and doubt they held the Hebrew people together by the bonds of absolute faith. Without the dynamic force and unquestioning belief of these men Judaism would probably have perished and Christianity would never have been born.

In 586 B.C. Nebuchadnezzar, Emperor of Babylon, stormed Jerusalem and laid waste the rest of the country. He carried off almost the entire population to captivity in Babylon, and Judea fell into ruin. This might have been the end of Judaism, but though Jewish exiles took part in Babylonian life, studied its art, and absorbed its learning, they rejected its gods. They brought up their children according to the Laws of Moses and the teachings of the prophets.

About fifty years later, King Cyrus of Persia captured Babylon and became master of a great empire. He readily agreed to release any Jews who wanted to return to Judea. By royal decree he sent them on their way and encouraged them to rebuild their devastated country. They were not daunted by this formidable task. With patient devotion they plowed up the barren fields, made new homes, and rebuilt the Temple. At this critical time a priest named Ezra gave Judaism a unity and inspiration that centuries of persecution have never been able to destroy.

The Laws of Moses had been set down in the first five books of the Old Testament in a series of scrolls known in Hebrew as the Torah, and later in Greek as the Pentateuch. Ezra summoned the people of Judea to Jerusalem and read the Torah to them. He told them what lay behind the laws and how they should be obeyed. Without them life had no meaning. The Laws of God regulated family life and business deals, work and recreation. They prescribed what people should learn and eat and wear. As the Judeans listened they felt secure and confident. They were the Chosen People with special guidance from the Lord. They were forbidden to mix with other nations, and they did not want to.

From all Judea they gathered every year at the Temple to celebrate three pilgrim festivals with solemn ritual. The first was the feast of the Passover, which lasted for seven days while the Children of Israel gave thanks for the birth of their nation at the exodus from Egypt. The second was the Festival of Weeks, or Pentecost, which in Jewish tradition is associated with the revelation on Mount Sinai.

The third feast was Sukkoth, when Jewish families lived for a whole week outside their houses in tents, or booths, to commemorate the forty years of wandering in the desert.

All these festivals were both religious and historical, marking God's special relationship with the Jewish people. In the autumn they celebrated the New Year, Rosh ha-Shanah, and gave thanks for the creation of the world.

Two centuries of comparative peace elapsed between the return from exile in Babylon and the next overwhelming invasion of Judea. In 332 B.C. Alexander the Great swept through the Middle East on his way to Egypt. Alexander was a fine general and a good statesman. He respected law and order and admired learning and he did not try to stamp out Judaism.

After the conquest a great many Jews emigrated to the city of Alexandria, attracted by the growing Greek scholarship and culture there. Their children grew up speaking Greek instead of Hebrew and lost touch with the scriptures. In 288 B.C., seventy learned scribes were summoned from Jerusalem to Alexandria to translate the Torah into Greek. The book which emerged from this mighty labor was called the Septuagint, and it was read throughout the civilized world.

But war went on, and about 170 B.C., Syrian invaders, bitter rivals of the ruling Greeks, stormed Jerusalem and set up a pagan altar in the Temple. Judas Maccabeus, son of an aged priest, raised a band of men who came to be known as the Maccabees and led them against the hated Syrians. The Maccabees fought with such skill and fury that in the year 142 B.C. the Jews were given their independence, which they retained for almost a hundred years. But in 63 B.C., Roman legions marched through the countries of the Middle East. Though Judea came under Roman rule, the stubborn spirit of revolt smoldered in the hearts of the Jewish people.

At times of adversity and deep despair, the prophets of Judea had foretold the coming of a Messiah to lead the nation to greater holiness and happiness. The people longed for a second David, and in the minds of many Jews the Messiah took the form of an earthly king endowed with heavenly power.

Under Roman rule, Jesus of Nazareth, the founder of Christianity, was born in Judea. He was brought up in the Jewish faith and traveled about the country as a preacher and healer. Jesus gathered a band of devoted followers who hailed him as the long-awaited Messiah. He died up the Cross because he refused to deny to the Jewish priests and the Roman Governor that he had been sent by God to save the world from sin. In the years following the death of Christ, many Jews refused to acknowledge him as the Messiah because they could not accept any other divine power than the Lord. Others recognized the divinity of Christ, and from this time onward Judaism and Christianity grew into separate religions.

In the first century after the death of Christ disaster struck Judea. The people of Jerusalem rebelled and the Romans decided to crush them once and for all. An army sacked the city and massacred thousands of Jews. The survivors were driven from their homes and exiled from the country. When the rebellion ended only one wall of the Temple remained standing. It is known as the Wailing Wall because so many Jews have since returned to Jerusalem to pray besides its ancient stones and bemoan the loss of their sanctuary.

In 70 A.D. it must have seemed to the scattered Jews that nothing was left of the state of Judea except its history. But in the previous centuries many families had moved from Palestine to Rome and Greece, as well as to Alexandria. They had formed reli-

The Wailing Wall in Jerusalem

gious communities, and after the destruction of Jerusalem they were joined by the Jews of the dispersal, a host of devout but penniless refugees. In the face of apparent disaster these exiles never lost hope, for they were sustained by the laws of the Torah and the certainty of protection from the God of Israel.

4 · *Hinduism – The Religion of India*

JUDAISM AND CHRISTIANITY have spread far beyond the borders of their native land. There are Christians and Jews of almost every nationality and the Bible and Torah have been translated into hundreds of languages. But Hinduism has remained the religion of India. Almost all the three hundred and ten million Hindus in the world today live in the country where their religion originated many thousand years ago.

The history of Hinduism is as old as the history of India. It did not have a single founder like Christianity, Buddhism, or Islam, but emerged slowly from ancient rites and customs, gathering inspiration from the sages and sacred literature of the centuries. There are many schools of thought and diverse sects in Hinduism; but they all maintain that every creature, human and animal, has an unchanging soul and that they die and are constantly reborn, forming one eternal span of life in a vast universe.

Recent excavations have shown that about 2500 B.C., when the Sumerians had settled by the Euphrates and the Egyptians were building a nation on the banks of the Nile, people were leading an equally ordered existence on the banks of the River Indus in the country that is now Pakistan. Scholars have been baffled by the script of this Indus Valley civilization, but the discovery of the towns of Harappa and Mohenjo Daro reveals a talent for architecture, agriculture, craftsmanship, and business equal to that of the Sumerians.

The people of this civilization lived in houses of brick and mud, they had bathrooms and a good drainage system, and they knew how to construct arches and domes. They planted cotton and wove it into cloth, mined gold and silver, and hunted elephants for their tusks. They carried on a thriving trade with other countries, and it is quite possible that some of Solomon's gold, ivory, apes, and peacocks came from the Indus Valley.

The Indus Valley way of life was disrupted by the arrival of hordes of fair-skinned people from the west. No one knows where they came from originally, but they evidently occupied Persia and then poured over the mountains with irresistible force about 1700 B.C. These warlike invaders had the name of Aryan, meaning "noble," which they used to distinguish themselves from the native peoples whom they considered an inferior race because of their darker color. They coined the word Hindu to describe the land east of the Indus River; so to begin with it applied to a country and later to a people and their faith.

As the Aryans did not know how to write they did not hand down detailed information about their early activities in India; but they seem to have behaved rather like the Norse Vikings who terrorized much of Europe in the ninth and tenth centuries after Christ. With spears and battle axes they conquered the surrounding tribes, settled down among them, and adapted Aryan customs to local conditions. They set to work to clear patches of forest and jungle to make pastures for their cows, and planted barley and other cereals.

The Aryans introduced Sanskrit at first as a spoken language. Later it became the language of scholarship in India and fulfilled the same purpose as Greek and Latin in the Western world. They also brought with them their own religion, and worshiped Varuna, god of sky and space; Indra, god of thunder and rain; Agni, god of fire; Surya, god of the sun, and many minor deities.

The Aryans built no temples, for it was fitting that the gods of nature should receive praise and homage in the open air. Priests lighted fires on sanctified sites and with elaborate ceremonial made offerings, at first human, and later of animals, grain, milk, and a drink called *soma*. Indra, the storm god, was believed to be most warlike and demanding and the people feared him before all others. They knew if he unleashed his tempests the land would be devastated and if he sealed up his rain clouds they would surely starve. Gradually holy men and magicians formed a set of beliefs and a code of laws that, they trusted, were acceptable to the gods and to men.

The seven hundred years of Indian history between 1500 and 800 B.C. are known as the Vedic Age. The name comes from the Sanskrit word *Veda,* or divine knowledge, which the Aryans believed was given out to certain men whom the gods considered worthy to interpret it to people on earth.

There is a later Hindu legend that the Vedic creator-god Brahma wrote it himself on leaves of gold.

There are four Vedas, or Collections of Knowledge, which together make up the sacred book of Hinduism. They are the fruits of long years of religious thought and study and are as precious to a Hindu as the Bible to a Christian. The Vedas are composed of psalms and hymns, rule and ritual, and philosophy mixed with magic. They do not, like the Bible, contain accounts of God's dealings with man, but rather of a growing revelation of God. Also they are not concerned with historic events, battles, floods, or famines. The most important of the four Vedas is the Rig-Veda, made up of 1,028 hymns of praise; the others contain a mass of information on music, sacrificial services, magic spells, and legends of the gods.

The art of writing had been lost with the Indus Valley civilization, and it was only re-introduced in another form about 800 B.C. when merchants brought a Semitic script from Western Asia. Even then the Hindus preferred to talk and sing rather than write. For a thousand years the Vedas were kept alive because they were recited from memory. The priests chanted them at religious ceremonies and sacrificial feasts. They also established centers of study and learning in remote places, far from worldly distractions. These religious schools became famous through the skill of their teachers and the standards of education. In just the same way that modern universities throughout the world attract pupils, students traveled long distances to sit at the feet of men who had won respect by their wisdom and holiness.

The sixth century B.C. was a time of intense religious activity, and a ferment of new thought welled up in India. Gradually the Hindu religion began to take shape, based on the Vedas and other forms of Aryan worship. The time had come when a number of Indians were no longer satisfied with legends about many different gods. They began to ponder deeply on the mysteries of the universe, seeking an explanation of the meaning of life. Many young men left their homes and went to live in the forests where they spent their time discussing the purpose of the world around them and the source of their being. They felt that there must be one eternal power, which they called Brahman, ever present and infinitely wise. They did not relate this divine presence to Brahma, the male god of Vedic times. Some of them thought of Brahman in the same way that people in Western countries think of God, as a supreme being with a personal responsibility for those who believe in him. Others were more mystical; they held that Brahman was beyond all description and all human understanding, the essence of life, the soul of the world, one with Atman, the inmost self within the heart of man. Whether Hindus thought of Brahman as a personal guardian or an eternal spiritual force, they all agreed that their salvation depended on merging with this omnipotent power. Only in this way could they be liberated from the ties of human existence.

The forest hermits recorded their teaching and the outcome of their discussions in a series of beautiful texts known as the Upanishads, which formed the last section of the Vedas. In the same way that Hinduism is a mixture of many faiths this mass of sacred literature contained the ideas of many pious and scholarly men trying to bring peace and comfort to a restless world.

They wrote also two magnificent epic poems, the *Mahabarata,* the longest poem in the world, and the *Ramayana.* The *Mahabarata* includes among its many verses the famous *Bhagavad Gita,* the Song of the Lord, now beautifully translated into both Eastern and Western languages. In the form of a heroic legend, the *Bhagavad Gita* expresses Hindu belief in one matchless presence and the bounden duty of every man to serve it.

These religious works also proclaim the Hindu principle of rebirth and accept the divisions of class, which have regulated the social structure of Indian life since time immemorial. Othodox Hindus believe that people are sent into the world at the will of a Creator who, armed with divine knowledge, places them exactly where they deserve to be. They also uphold the doctrine that every living being is fitted into a universal plan; that both humans and animals are graded according to their good or bad behavior in a former life, and that once they are born no power on earth can change their status until they die. They must remain at the same social level from the cradle to the grave, conform to the rules of caste, and be content. This is the Law of Karma.

Orthodox Hindus aim to ascend the ladder of earthly success step by step through virtue and self-sacrifice until they earn eternal rest in union with God. Their hope of promotion lies not in the present life but in the next. An honest and hardworking peasant seeks his reward in the distant future. He looks forward to rebirth in a higher caste with better social standing and easier living conditions. On the other hand Hindus know that sin will surely be punished, and a murderer or thief may well eke out a miserable next existence as a pig or a rat.

There were originally four main social classes in India: the Brahmans, who were priests and scholars; the princes, warriors, and aristocrats; the merchants and farmers; and the laborers and servants. The four classes were divided into thousands of castes, each with its own marriage customs, crafts, and tribal traditions. The restrictions of caste are today more important to the ordinary man than those of class, though marriage between men and women of different classes is still discouraged.

In the early days of Hinduism the highest class, the Brahmans, gained immense power and many privileges. They have been guardians of religion and scholarship ever since, esteemed for their holiness and knowledge, responsible for leading the people in prayer and upholding the traditions of the Vedas.

The members of the second class were of noble birth, rajas and kings and headmen of tribes, or descendants of military families who followed in their ancestors' footsteps. These Indian rulers came from many different races and spoke different languages. They governed states from the snow-covered Himalayas to the steaming plains by the Indian Ocean. They fought for supremacy but none of them succeeded in conquering all India. The one common link was their class. It gave, and still gives them, a particular position and a prestige which their people acknowledge and understand.

The situation in the third class is very different. A mechanized age, new skills, wider learnings, and a national need to develop the country have opened up thousands of jobs outside trade and farming. The men and women who are qualified to fill them are very valuable and neither they nor their employers are greatly troubled by class and caste restrictions. These young Hindus work in politics, medicine, law, teaching, banking, business, engineering, and every other profession that a developing nation offers. They belong to caste councils which are rather like trade unions, designed to defend the rights of their members, and they live by their brains and ability rather than their birthright.

However, the peasant men and women who until very recently formed a fourth vast uneducated class near the bottom of the social scale are still struggling to break through a wall of ancient prejudice and restraint. More of their children go to school each year, but they often fail to get the higher education which would give them a profession. When they leave they are forced to take the same kind of jobs that their fathers and mothers did before them.

From the beginning of Hinduism there has always been in India a group of unfortunate people who belong to no class at all and live in a state of pathetic poverty at the lowest level of human existence. They are known as outcastes, or untouchables, and they work as scavengers, butchers, and executioners, jobs that are considered unclean and contemptible. These outcastes come from small tribes, defeated and dominated by stronger neighbors, or from families which have fallen on evil days through some major misfortune. They used to be banned from any form of contact with people who belonged to one of the

Pilgrims bathe in the River Ganges at Benares

four great classes. They were not allowed to draw water from a
public well or bathe in the Ganges or any other holy river, so
they could not wash; schools would not accept outcaste children, so they were hopelessly ignorant; and they were forbidden
to enter a temple so they could find no consolation in religion.

When an outcaste went shopping he had to shout his needs from afar and put the money down. Then he retreated a certain distance, dictated by the caste laws, and stole back later to pick up the goods. If, by mischance, the shadow of an untouchable fell on Hindus of caste they had to be purified by a special cleansing ceremony before they could continue their ordinary lives.

Expanding education and increasing land, sea, and air transport are gradually undermining ancient tradition. When Indians learn to read and have a chance to travel, they are able to compare conditions in India with those in other countries and question the justice of everlasting inequality. Hindu reformers are aware of the need to revise long-standing laws. In many regions temples and shops have been opened to outcastes. But the caste system has been the cornerstone of Hindu religious and social life for so long that it would be dangerous to sweep it away with revolutionary speed.

Because of the basic Hindu belief that men and women can be reborn as animals, Hindus are reluctant to kill any animal for fear of causing pain to a human soul. Many Hindus do not eat meat, and the Jains, an extreme sect which broke away from Hinduism, will not harm a poisonous snake or crush a mosquito.

Hindus have great respect for monkeys and snakes, but above all other animals they pay homage to cows and bulls. Gilded images of them appear in temples and household shrines. In real life they are cherished, petted, and allowed to wander wherever they wish and nibble whatever they fancy. It is a terrible sin to injure one of them, and most Hindus would rather starve than eat beef.

As India itself is a mixture of peoples, so Hinduism is a storehouse of their ideas and customs. It is in general a tolerant religion, rather undemanding. Powerful as the Brahmans are, they have never tried to impose a universal creed or set of religious rules on the whole Hindu community. Hinduism is more a way of life than a manner of worship. Hindus do not unite to persecute new sects, and ritual varies from region to region and family to family. The laws of caste regulate how people shall behave, not precisely what they shall believe. Hindus consider that the greatest virtues are kindness, truthfulness, and love, and that men should choose their own paths to holiness. They may approach God by way of knowledge, hard work, or sacrifice and prayer.

The Hindu ideal is a state of utter selflessness and some try to attain it through practicing Yoga. Through a rigid course of self-discipline they learn to control their minds and senses. Step by step they strive to free their souls from earthly ties and their bodies from physical feeling. Some exhibit their prowess in public by walking on hot coals without flinching or cutting their skin without bleeding, others spend their lives in ceaseless meditation. These Yogis are among the holy men of Hinduism. A number of them sit immobile in crowded places, blind to the noise and bustle around them, but thousands more live like hermits in unbroken solitude. They give up all their possessions, depending on gifts of food for bare subsistence, and they are deeply respected because of their holiness. By casting aside everything that the world has to offer, they hope to atone for their sins, and many of them die by an act of willpower when they have completed their self-imposed penance.

There are Hindu ceremonies for every social and historic occasion and all the seasons. Special days are set aside to honor the various gods. Most temples hold yearly festivals when their own particular god is mounted on an elephant or carried aloft through the streets in a spectacular procession. Often people combine religious services with cattle markets and the harvest. Sometimes the ritual of the celebrations is so ancient that it has entirely lost its original meaning. Brahman priests officiate at certain established feasts in stately surroundings, but in country places groups of ordinary people hold simple services for local gods who they feel are sympathetic to their particular problems.

The real center of Hinduism is in the home. There are sacraments for every stage in the life of a human being, from the months preceding birth to the period of mourning after death, and almost all Hindu families observe them. It is a religious event when a child is conceived, born, and weaned from its mother's breast. When a high-class Hindu boy reaches his teens, a priest instructs him in religious duties and, with solemn ritual, places a sacred thread over his right shoulder. This is a symbol of second birth and the boy must wear it until he dies.

Marriage is the focal point of Hindu life. Husbands and wives long for children, particularly sons, to support them in their old age and conduct the funeral services. In former times polygamy, or multi-marriage, was an accepted custom, particularly when the first wife was childless.

Child marriage was another ancient Hindu practice. It is only in this generation that girls have had a voice in selecting their husbands. Previously it was customary for their parents to choose a suitable boy of the same caste. When the girl was ten or twelve years old, the marriage ceremony took place with the most lavish display that the family could possibly afford. Once the wedding feast was over, the little bride returned to her home until she was old enough to have children. Then she joined her husband and settled down to serve him faithfully for the rest of her life. Until quite recently, if a boy or a man died, his widow or widows were forbidden to marry again for fear of complications in the afterlife. It was a cruel fate for little girls who lost husbands they hardly knew to face perpetual widowhood.

The Indian custom of *suttee,* a Sanskrit word meaning "true" or "loyal," demanded a supreme sacrifice from a high-class Hindu woman. If a husband died, his widows were expected to accompany him to the funeral pyre and to be cremated by his side. Probably the practice arose from a Hindu ideal that happily married people should never be separated and therefore should proceed together to the next life. The practice of *suttee* gradually declined and in 1829 was finally declared illegal.

The position of women in India has varied with the times they lived in. In the Vedic Age they enjoyed personal freedom and near-equality with men. But in the eighth century after Christ's birth, Moslem armies invaded India from the west and during the next four hundred years overran much of the country. Hindu husbands had always been strict with their wives, but after the Moslems came they gave them even less freedom. Soon a system of *purdah,* a Persian word meaning "curtain," prevailed throughout the Moslem and Hindu world. Married women were so secluded that they were completely cut off from normal life. They appeared in public heavily veiled, and only their husbands and sons were ever allowed to see their faces. Even the family doctor had to treat his women patients from the other side of a curtain.

Until the twentieth century, Indian women, with the exception of a few of high degree, had no education at all. No one thought it necessary for them to know anything outside their household duties and how to keep their husbands happy. Even the fortunate few who could read and write took no part in public life.

The outlook is different in India today. Female education is far from universal, but the girls who get it can use their training and talent to the full. The legal marriage age has been raised to fourteen years and many girls choose their own husbands. In 1966 Mrs. Indira Gandhi, daughter of the late prime minister Jawaharlal Nehru, was elected prime minister of India.

Religious building in India began on a big scale in the last centuries B.C. At this time also, the fabulous resources of the country were revealed. Miners discovered rare metals and precious stones and Indian craftsmen learned how to use them. Provincial rulers grew rich on the proceeds of timber, ivory, and spices. They carried jeweled swords and ate off plates of gold. Their crowns were heavy with emeralds and diamonds, rubies and pearls; and even their elephants wore golden trappings. These wealthy chiefs and warriors built castles for their own defense,

Hindu temple at Mylapore in India

and dressed their many wives in gleaming silks and finest cotton, embroidered with gold thread. They also constructed beautiful temples to their gods.

For the first time, Hindu temples were built of stone instead of brick and clay. The roofs were encrusted with thousands of mystical figures and the altars decorated with carved images of many gods. Foremost among them was Vishnu, the preserver, whom Hindus believe descends at intervals in a number of different forms from heaven, where he reigns supreme, to look after people on earth. He has appeared through the ages as a fish, a tortoise, a boar, a dwarf, a heroic warrior, and finally as the Buddha. Vishnu is always kind and good, but Siva, the second great god of Hinduism, has a grim side to his nature. He is a destroyer, and lurks on battlefields and in the vicinity of corpses. Sometimes he is dancing but he often wears a garland of skulls and is attended by evil spirits. At the same time he is also worshiped as a god of meditation, and for his power to encourage fertility in man and beast.

Kali, the wife of Siva, is a mother goddess, also with a dual personality, either fierce or fond. Siva's son, the elephant-headed Ganesh, is a popular god, a gay carrier of good luck, usually presented with six heads and twelve arms, riding on a peacock.

These deities have largely displaced Brahma and the other Vedic gods. Though they vary in relative importance from one province to another, Hindus believe that they work as one with Brahman, the eternal power, controlling the universe. Around them in the spirit world are millions of lesser gods, each with its own image in the temples. Hindu priests do not condemn what

The dancing god Siva

to people of other faiths seems to be outright idolatry. They feel that the conception of one high God as creator and preserver of the whole universe is too complex and remote for low-caste Hindus to grasp, and that through simpler and more approachable gods they may find their way to him.

In the tenth century in Northern India, a teacher named Nanak denounced idolatry and the caste system. He blended the beliefs of Hinduism and Islam and preached of one universal God for all men. His followers are known as Sikhs, or disciples, and in their golden temple at Amritsar, a gleaming shrine set in the center of a lovely lake, there are no idols. The Sikhs have become a militant sect, noted for their bravery. They take vows never to turn their backs in battle and always carry a two-edged dagger. They are forbidden to cut their hair or shave their faces. They wear twisted turbans and long beards as an outward mark of their faith, and to distinguish them from people of other sects in India and the Far East.

In the same way that the Nile was held in reverence by the early Egyptians, the Ganges has been, for untold centuries, the holy river of India. It rises in the Himalayas and flows for fifteen hundred miles to the Bay of Bengal. At intervals along the river banks there are *ghats,* an Indian word for steps, sacred sites where millions of pilgrims come every year to wash away their sins in the holy waters, cure their bodily ills, or burn the bodies of their dead. Some are well-to-do Hindus who make the journey without undue sacrifice; but many are very poor indeed, living at just above starvation level, and they deprive themselves of the bare necessities of life to reach the Ganges once before they die.

The holy city of Benares is the center of Hindu pilgrimage. It lies on a curling crescent of the great river, with golden-roofed temples and shrines rising tier upon tier above the broad *ghats* which line the water's edge. At dawn and in the evening the *ghats* are crowded with trusting Hindus who fearfully bring their sinful souls and ailing bodies to the healing waters.

Hindu funeral rites have changed little from primitive times. In the Vedic Age, corpses were regarded with suspicion and fear. They were unclean and unlucky and no one dared to offend the gods and goddesses of the earth by burying them in a grave. This superstition has persisted, and family mourners still build funeral pyres of wood fagots and burn their dead as quickly as possible. When the flesh is consumed by the fire, the bones are cast into a river. The relatives are tainted by their association with the dead, and for ten days they are also unclean. They shave their heads and stay at home offering up prayers and food to the spirit of the departed. This period of family devotion is intended to bridge the gulf between one life and the next and prepare the way for rebirth. It is one of the main reasons that parents are in despair if they are childless, for then they have no one they can count on to look after them when they die.

During the last hundred years a new spirit has entered into Hinduism. There are still many million orthodox Hindus who remain unquestioningly faithful to ancient belief and ritual. At the same time there are a growing number of thoughtful Indians who respect traditional teaching, but find that they cannot apply certain parts of it to modern life. Many of these men are working with the government to give their people greater social justice within the framework of Hindu faith. Child marriage, the burning of widows, and polygamy are now illegal. Animal sacrifice is less common than it used to be, and the outcastes are beginning to share the rights of other Indians.

This new Hinduism and the social ideals that go with it spread through the country under the enlightened leadership of Mahatma Gandhi, one of the greatest men in Hindu history. He was born in 1869, at a time when nationalism was awakening in Asian countries. Gandhi was a deeply religious man with high political principles, and he had a profound influence, not only on the educated classes, but also on the simple people. They revered him as a saint and loved him as a master. He taught Hindus to respect other faiths as well as their own. He absorbed Christian and Moslem teachings and molded them to the Hindu point of view so that his own people could understand them. He spoke of a god of truth and love. Gandhi worked for Indian freedom, but he always preached non-violence, and he lived to see his country proclaim its independence from nearly two hundred years of British rule.

In 1947 India, forerunner among the new nations, was divided into two states each with its own independent government and its own religion: India where the majority of people are Hindu, and Pakistan where they are almost all Moslem. In January 1948, because of his belief in religious toleration, Gandhi was murdered by a fanatical Hindu who accused him of trying to bring Hindus and Moslems closer together. The example of

Division of Hindu and Moslem religions

Gandhi's life and the tragedy of his death opened the eyes of the world to the power and the passion of the Hindu religion. At the same time Hindu writers and spokesmen began to present their faith to the Western world as a religious force to be reckoned with in the future outside the frontiers of India.

5 · A New Light in the East

TWO THOUSAND FIVE HUNDRED years ago on the northeastern frontier of India, in the region that is now Nepal, a king named Shuddhodhana ruled over a small mountainous domain. He was chieftain of the proud Sakya tribe, and his people were hardy and independent. His palace was situated on the foothills of the towering Himalayas, overlooking the plain where the River Ganges flowed southeastward past the holy city of Benares to the sea.

Shuddhodhana was a Hindu and a member of the warrior class. For a long time he had no children, but about the year 560 B.C. a prince was born amidst great rejoicing. The baby was called Siddhartha and many different legends have grown up telling of a miraculous birth and exceptional childhood. He was brought up with other young nobles of his class, trained in the art of war, and educated by the sages. He was an able student and excelled in sport. At the age of sixteen Siddhartha won a beautiful wife in a contest of arms and when she presented him with a son his happiness seemed to be complete.

Life at court was pleasant and luxurious, though in the countryside beyond the palace walls there was poverty and pain.

Shuddhodhana did everything he could to shield his son from the troubled world, but the young prince grew restless. He rode out among the people and saw for the first time a very old man, shrunken and frail. Then he passed a man suffering from plague and crying out in agony. Finally he met a party of weeping mourners, bearing a corpse to the funeral pyre.

Siddhartha was deeply disturbed and filled with compassion. He decided to go out into the world to look for the cause of this sadness and suffering so that he could help his fellow men. One night he said good-by to his wife and young son while they were sleeping, and secretly left the palace. At first he turned to the religious hermits in the forest for advice, but they could not satisfy his quest for knowledge. Then Siddhartha tried to reach the truth through fasting and prayer. He reduced his food to the point of starvation, but he soon realized that his mind was blurred with hunger and he was making no progress. So he began to eat normally again and to think more clearly. He spent his time in constant meditation, seeking a solution for the ills of the world.

For seven years, Siddhartha sought wisdom to cure the troubles and sorrows of mankind. Suddenly one day, while he was sitting beneath the spreading branches of a pepal tree, sheltered from the intense heat of the Indian sun, his long search ended in a tremendous spiritual experience. Almost in a flash he gained the enlightenment he had been looking for and the way to salvation opened up before him.

From this time onward Siddhartha was known to his followers as the Buddha, the Awakened or Enlightened One.

They did not regard him as a god, or credit him with divine power, but believed that by his unwavering resolution he had found complete understanding and attained extreme goodness. They tried to follow his example and cast off worldly ties and temptations, knowing that only this absolute detachment would lead them to the state of timeless bliss which the Buddha called Nirvana.

To Buddhists Nirvana takes the place of Brahman to Hindus. Buddhists believe that three other living men have previously discovered the Truth and taught it as Buddhas, and that there is yet one more to come. It is universally recognized, however, that it was Siddhartha, also known as Gautama Sakaymuni, who founded the Buddhist faith and set out to spread it among his fellow men.

He preached his first sermon in the Deer Park of Sarnath, near the city of Benares, and immediately won five faithful disciples. The Buddha told them that the pain and sorrow of mankind were due to false values and a selfish craving for worldly things which would crumble and decay. He told them too that ignorance was the greatest of all evils because it meant wrong thinking, and it could only be stamped out by true understanding. The Buddha based his teaching on Four Noble Truths: the existence of Pain, the cause of Pain, the need to avoid the cause of Pain, and the way of ending Pain by the Noble Eightfold Path. The Eightfold Path is a pattern for pure and perfect living: right outlook, right resolve, right speaking, right conduct, right livelihood, right effort, right mindfulness, and right concentration.

The Buddha believed in self-discipline, but also in moderation. The Way he taught was not an easy one, but he did not go to extremes and prescribe long fasts and excessive physical strain. He urged his disciples to seek a middle road between easygoing indulgence and self-imposed hardship. His Eightfold Path was a practical path to purity. He was convinced that if people could really understand the importance of the Four Truths they would stop longing for selfish things, they would no longer be jealous or cruel, and would have no desire to kill or steal or behave badly. They would earn their living in a way that was not harmful to others, and would keep their bodies healthy and their minds clear. They would learn to concentrate on things that were good and to meditate deeply. Thus they would find deliverance from self and cease to exist except in Nirvana.

The Buddha agreed with the Hindu conception of repeated rebirth but he did not acknowledge the existence of an unchanging human soul, and of an eternal self condemned to follow an inevitable course from one life to the next. He rejected the caste system because he believed it was possible for everyone to follow in the way which he prescribed, and he denied that the course of a man's whole life was determined by the conditions of his birth. The Buddha believed that people are simply links in the Wheel of Life; that they are born, live, and die according to the laws of nature, as a seed lies in the ground and becomes a plant, as a river rises in the mountains and flows to the sea, and as snow falls and melts away. But at the same time he claimed that human beings were responsible for their own salvation.

The moral teachings of the Buddha are very similar to the

Commandments of Moses. Buddha told his lay followers: do not harm or kill the lowest living creature; give freely and receive gratefully, but do not seize by force or fraud; speak the truth because a lie hurts most of all the liar; do not drink alcohol because it clouds the mind; and be faithful to marriage vows. Buddhism is a manner of living transformed into a religion through reverence for its founder. The Buddha did not openly reject Hindu gods but he bypassed them. He acknowledged their existence, but not their importance. He presented no rival gods, nor did he dictate to people how they should worship. He simply told them the way to live and gave them a target to work for. It was in fact a target of personal perfection combining kindliness, pity, joy, and inner quietness.

Siddhartha lived at a time when many Hindus were challenging ancient beliefs and examining the existing order of life. He was evidently an eloquent preacher and his words made a deep impression.

Gradually an Order of Buddhist monks and nuns was formed, dedicated to the teaching of the Master. They worked in strictly regulated communities and were forbidden to marry. It is said of the monks that "their heads were shaven and their souls serene." Their worldly possessions were limited to three garments, besides a sash, an alms bowl, a razor, a needle, and a water strainer. Their quarters were bare and they were permitted only one meal a day between nine and ten in the morning. The saffron-yellow robes of the Buddhist Order became a familiar sight in Indian towns and villages. The words of the Buddha brought comfort and hope to a people haunted by superstitious fear of angry gods, and the monks and nuns made many converts.

Individual goodness is an essential part of Buddhism. The Buddha set an outstanding example in his own life and insisted that the members of his Order did likewise. Their daily round was made up of study, contemplation, and good works. They collected alms, recited the Buddha's teachings, learned from their seniors, and instructed their juniors in his words and his works. They went out into the towns and the country and preached to laymen, always stressing the importance of human relationships: parent to child, master to servant, teacher to pupil, and neighbor to neighbor. They extolled the eight Buddhist virtues of love, truth, self-respect, chastity, humility, charity, compassion, holiness, and cheerful submission to misfortune. A convert had to make three promises:

> I take my refuge in the Buddha
> I take my refuge in the *Dhamma* (Teaching)
> I take my refuge in the *Sangha* (Order)

For forty-five years the Buddha traveled through northern India, constantly spreading the Truths that had been revealed to him. At the urgent request of his aged father, he returned to his native land where he was received with rapture and reverence by his countrymen. They were readily converted to Buddhist doctrines and the great teacher received his own son into the Order. But despite the pleas of his family he would not remain with them, for his work was unfinished.

At the age of eighty the Buddha died, surrounded by his devoted disciples. It is said that after his body was burned the ashes were divided and sent to the kings, princes, and rajas in those countries where he had lived and taught. They were enshrined as most sacred relics and visited by adoring pilgrims.

The Buddha's words and his deeds were handed down by word of mouth from one generation to another. It is inevitable that they took on new shades of meaning according to the character of the narrator. Some centuries after the Buddha's death, they were brought together in one collection, known as the Pali Canon, because it was inscribed on dried palm leaves in Pali, an ancient language which has since died out. At about the same time the Buddha's teaching was also set down in Sanskrit.

Little is known of the progress of Buddhism between the death of the founder in about 480 B.C. and the conquest of northwestern India by Alexander the Great in 326 B.C. Following his usual habit, Alexander did not interfere with the religion of the country. He subdued the native rulers one by one, appointed a governor to collect tribute from them, and returned to the West. His empire soon outgrew its strength and he did not have sufficient forces to establish anything but nominal control in the parts of India which he conquered. When he died at the early age of thirty-three, an ambitious Indian warrior named Chandragupta Maurya raised an army, overthrew Alexander's skeleton government, and took the power into his own hands. He soon captured most of India, for only the extreme south managed to stand out against him.

About 270 B.C., Asoka, grandson of Chandragupta, inherited the throne. He is the most celebrated of all Indian emperors, outstanding for the courage of his convictions. He began his reign as a ruthless warrior and, before he died, earned the reputation of a saint. When he came to the throne, he ruled by violence according to the customs of his age. He was unsparing in his revenge against those who opposed or offended him until he was converted to Buddhism. From that day onward, Asoka turned from war to peace and did everything within his power to promote the Buddhist faith. He ordered giant stone pillars to be inscribed with royal edicts proclaiming Buddhism as a living faith. He set up one of these Rock Edicts at Sarnath where the Buddha preached his first sermon, and others in different parts of the empire to encourage people to embrace Buddhism. Asoka also financed schools, hospitals, and thousands of monasteries from his own treasury. He planted avenues of trees to shelter pilgrims on their way to Buddhist shrines, and built infirmaries to care for sick men and animals. By his own rule he set an example of toleration, piety, and compassion. Buddhism had always been a missionary faith, but Asoka enlarged the field, for he sent monks as far as Syria, Egypt, and Greece.

There is little evidence of religious art and architecture in India before the reign of Asoka, but from the third century B.C. onward, Buddhists, Hindus, and later, Moslems, created monuments of enduring loveliness. The Buddhists first built *stupas*, memorial towers, containing the ashes of the Buddha, where millions of pilgrims came to pay homage. Early Buddhist temples and monasteries were mostly on mountainsides or overlooking sacred rivers, cut out of the solid rock with infinite labor. Their deep cavernous recesses, pillared halls, and vaulted galleries are mysterious and impressive. These rock buildings were fol-

Demons guard a Buddhist temple in Thailand

lowed by temples and tombs of both brick and stone, constructed above ground and growing more elaborate as the centuries passed. The walls and the rooftops are adorned with symmetrical designs and sacred figures, the towers crowned with pineapple-shaped spires. Graceful gateways lead to golden shrines, and many temples encircle pepal, now called *bodhi*, trees in sacred memory of the Buddha's glorious moment of enlightenment beneath their shady branches.

About a century after the death of the Buddha, differences of opinion had arisen within the Buddhist Order, and by the reign of Asoka it was divided into two main schools of thought and a number of diverse minor sects. One of the two major divisions of Buddhism was strictly conservative, holding firmly to the original doctrines of the founder. This was the School of the Elders, or Theravada, and its monks continue today to instruct their pupils in the Four Noble Truths and the Eightfold Path to Nirvana, following word for word the instructions of the Buddha. They honor him as an inspired teacher, the founder of their faith, and the greatest of the three great Buddhas who have discovered the Truth and shown the way to salvation. They do not however worship him as a god. The Theravada tradition proclaims that those who follow the Buddhist Path need no spiritual help or guidance. The layman must go as far as he can along the road to perfection, and the monks must strive even harder to fulfill every condition of saintliness.

The second emerging school of thought was the Mahayana. The name stands for the Greater Vehicle to Salvation, and because its members were so sure that their interpretation of the

Distribution of Buddhist sects

Buddha's teaching was the right one, they looked down upon the rival school and called it Hinayana, or the Lesser Vehicle to Salvation. Mahayana Buddhists have broadened their beliefs into a revised version of the original doctrines. They put their trust in the value of spiritual faith as well as personal effort. They maintain that men can win salvation by good works and a

pure life, and also by seeking heavenly aid. They have transformed the Buddha, the teacher, into an eternal glorified being
endowed with divine power, approaching man in many different
forms. They declare that the Buddha works through *bodhisattvas,*
or savior Buddhas, virtuous people who have reached a state of
complete understanding. Some *bodhisattvas* stay in Nirvana
working for universal goodness; but others voluntarily give up
the celestial positions which they have earned by their unwavering
resolve and return to earth striving for the redemption of
mankind.

Besides the *bodhisattvas* Mahayana Buddhists recognize
another class of savior beings, or blessed ones, who dwell in the
heavens and minister to the needs of man. These are Dhyani
Buddhas, contemplative and thoughtful, and they wear the simple
garments of a monk, in contrast to the *bodhisattvas* who are
always represented in princely dress. Outstanding among the
Dhyani Buddhas is Amitabha, for he has become one of the
great gods of Asia, known in China as O-mi-to, and in Japan as
Amida. The many followers of Amitabha belong to the Pure
Land Sect, for they believe that he presides over a paradise which
they call the Land of Bliss, or Pure Land, where infinite light
prevails. Their ultimate aim is to reach this ideal heaven by
means of true faith. They honor Amitabha by devout repetition
of his name and trust that he will welcome all who have faith in
him and grant them future bliss.

The Mahayana school was more expansive and speculative
than the Theravada and therefore less united. While Theravada
teachers kept faithfully to one body of scripture, the Pali Canon,

Mahayana teachers gathered groups of followers and preached new interpretations of the Buddha's early doctrines. When Theravada missionaries traveled abroad, they kept their faith intact, but when Mahayana missionaries encountered foreign religions, they viewed them tolerantly and sometimes combined them with their own beliefs.

In India, the Mahayana school reached its most influential peak in the first centuries after the Christian era, and in a host of scriptures expressed its newly discovered ecstasy and showed the fruits of profound research. Later, these scriptures were translated into other languages and found their way into the religious literature of China, Tibet, and Japan. As Mahayana Buddhists divided into different sects, they adopted scriptures fitting their own manner of worship.

In order to broaden its appeal and gain even greater support, Mahayana priests introduced images of the Buddha and great Buddhist teachers and savior beings, or saints, into the temples. In the way that portraits and statues of Christian saints differ according to the race and nationality of the artist or sculptor, the face and figure of the Buddha vary in appearance from one country to another. Only his absolute serenity remains constant and universal. When images were also set up in Hindu temples, Hinduism became confused with Buddhism in the minds of the mass of uneducated people. Many turned to Hinduism because it had less discipline and more outward attraction. Little by little, Buddhist monks lost their hold on Indian communities and moved into surrounding countries. The Mahayanans went northward to Tibet, China, Korea, and finally

Japan. The Theravadans established their faith in Ceylon, Burma, and Siam.

During the seventh century of the Christian era, Mahayana monks crossed the almost insurmountable barrier of the Himalayas and entered the country of Tibet. Living on a high windswept plateau, walled in by mountain ranges, the Tibetan people had had little contact with the outside world. They accepted Buddhism wholeheartedly, and adapted it to suit their own character and conditions. First in the capital of Lhasa, and then throughout the country, they built monasteries and temples. Men and women flocked to these religious centers until a sixth of the entire population was enrolled in Buddhist Orders.

Tibet has been called the Land of the Lamas, and this special form of Buddhism is known as Lamaism. Lama means "superior one," a title originally held by heads of monasteries and other senior dignitaries, but later adopted by monks of many ranks. High above them all stood the Dalai Lama, a priest-king revered by his people as a great saint of India constantly reborn in Tibet. Each divine ruler was chosen as a small boy from Tibetan families, regardless of social class. On his deathbed a Dalai Lama defined the nature of his successor, and oracles went out to find a child who had been born at the very moment the Dalai Lama died and was also possessed of the essential mystical powers. Sometimes the quest lasted for months; but once the court officials made their choice, they brought the boy to Lhasa and trained him carefully for the majestic position he was destined to occupy. At the age of sixteen a Dalai Lama was enthroned and thereafter reigned supreme until he died.

Tibetan lamas blow their prayer horns

This unique religious leadership lasted until 1951 when Tibet was taken over by Communist China. In 1959, the Tibetans revolted against Chinese rule, and the Dalai Lama, threatened by Communist retaliation, secretly crossed the frontier and sought refuge in India. The long reign of the Dalai Lamas is broken, and religion is ceasing to be the main force in Tibetan life. Under Communist rule the power of the religious orders is declining and the future of Lamaism is overcast with uncertainty.

Wherever Buddhists worship and whatever tradition or sect they belong to, they all claim that they are following the Buddha's Path, and that their goal is the same as his: enlightenment and timeless bliss in Nirvana. There is today a Pan Buddhist movement afoot, and in the same way that many churchmen are working for Christian unity a number of Buddhist leaders are aiming to erase the differences which separate the Mahayana and Theravada schools of thought and bring them closer together.

6 · The Religions of China

NORTH AND EAST of India stretches a vast territory now known as the People's Republic of China. There are today approximately seven hundred million Chinese, far more than any other people of a single nationality in the world. They are inheritors of an ancient civilization and three closely connected religions: Confucianism, Taoism, and Buddhism. Whereas most people in the Western world adopt one faith, a great many Chinese profess, to some extent, the doctrines of all these three.

Chinese civilization goes back to at least 2000 B.C., and in these early times the people worshiped a host of deities ranging from the Supreme Ruler of Heaven down to thousands of local gods. These celestial spirits were ever-present and extremely powerful. Some were tender and gracious, others spiteful and demanding. Most important of all were the spirits of family ancestors, and people consulted them constantly. Ancestor worship is a traditional Chinese cult, founded on the firm belief that ancestral spirits form an essential link between a living family and eternity.

It is probable that the Chinese people are made up of races from many parts of Asia, and it is known that by 1400 B.C., the most prosperous among them were living in timber-built houses, and employing artisans to work in gold and bronze, and carve in wood, jade, stone, and ivory. By this time a Chinese writing had developed, quite different from the scripts in Europe and Western Asia. Whereas Sumerian, Greek, and Hebrew letters stood for sounds, Chinese characters formed a kind of picture writing representing objects and ideas. At first scribes scratched them on bone and tortoise-shell; later, they painted them on bamboo, parchment, and silk with the delicate strokes of a fine brush. Chinese characters have changed less than other ancient writing, so it is not difficult to decipher them today.

The earliest records relate that about two thousand years before the Christian era, feudal warlords ruled the various provinces, fighting continually among themselves for supremacy. In the twelfth century B.C., the Chou family defeated rival chieftains with fearful bloodshed, and established a dynasty which lasted for the next nine hundred years. Chou kings built a capital in Shensi province, on the Yellow River, and collected tribute from lesser lords in the surrounding regions. Their territories included the silk province of Lu, which is now Shantung.

There was widespread violence and injustice under the Chou rulers. Long-suffering peasant armies fought to keep them in power, but the soldiers and their families had little share in the fruits of victory. Feudal landlords wore fur-lined coats in winter and silken robes in summer, and rode through the countryside in carriages decorated with gold and jade, drawn by prancing horses from the Mongolian plains. Their serfs, when they were not engaged in battle, worked as forced labor on farms and silkworm estates and wore rags. Flood, drought, and famine were common disasters.

In the sixth century B.C., new ideas were stirring in many lands and ardent reformers were pleading for government by humanity and reason instead of by brute force. Within a single century in India the Buddha taught that only a virtuous life leads to salvation; in Judea the prophets of Israel called for righteous living in the service of a righteous God; in Greece learned philosophers tried to unravel the tangled meaning of the universe; and in China Confucius, a wise and far-seeing scholar, struggled to create family harmony, national order, and world peace.

Confucius was born in Lu in 551 B.C., son of an impoverished nobleman who died when the boy was three years old. Confucius married at nineteen and had a son, but the marriage was an unhappy one and he divorced his wife. He could not afford an expensive education, and his knowledge of statecraft, history, and human relations was largely self-taught. He chose teaching as a career for himself and the best means of improving the hard lot of the common people. Traveling from province to province, he constantly denounced the injustice and brutality of the Chou government.

Confucius gathered around him a band of eager students. He studied the character of each and tried to bring out the best in them. He encouraged them to do well, not for their own sake, but for the good of the community. He gave them everyday rules for ordinary living, and spoke to them in simple words: "Virtue is to love men. And wisdom is to understand men."

The great teacher summed up for his pupils the wisdom of the ancient Chinese scholars and the experience of past generations. Ancestor worship existed in China long before Confucius' day, and he built his teaching around it. He told children to obey their parents and honor their ancestors, for a Chinese family is made up not only of living members, but also of those who have died but are ever-present in spirit.

He believed that a happy home was the basis of civilization, and that a family which was loving, loyal, and united could influence society as a whole. Because he regarded sincerity, wisdom, humanity, and courage as the highest virtues, he referred to a man who possessed them as a gentleman. Before Confucius' day the term only applied to nobility of birth, but he changed its meaning to describe nobility of character. He had a profound admiration for learning, and insisted that education was the natural right of all men. As a result of Confucius' guidance the Chinese people have, through the ages, shown far greater admiration for their scholars than their soldiers, and parents have not encouraged their sons to join the army. Confucius stressed the importance of setting a good example, and predicted that a just sovereign would be rewarded by an orderly kingdom and a virtuous father by happy children.

At the age of fifty-one the learned sage became prime minister of Lu; but when he discovered that the ruler refused to carry out the reforms that were so urgently needed, he resigned in disgust and went back to teaching. He offered the people no gods, ordained no clergy, built no churches and set down no creed. But he was filled with a sense of mission, and believed in the existence of a heaven and that goodness was immortal.

Confucius did not consider himself the founder of a faith, and it was only after his death that his message grew into a religion. His followers have tried to build an ideal state based on human kindness and worldly wisdom. The temples erected to his memory contain no portraits or statues, but simple tablets inscribed with his name.

Schoolboys in Formosa celebrate Confucius' birthday

In 136 B.C., the teaching of Confucius was proclaimed the official doctrine of the state and his standards were adopted as a national way of life. A state university was founded to train men in the principles of sound government. Until this time the mandarins (government officials) who administered the country had always come from noble families. The new university was open to rich and poor alike, and graduates were selected for responsible posts after a competitive examination on the teachings of Confucius. For the first time government jobs were awarded for merit instead of being handed out automatically to aristocratic applicants who might have no qualifications but their background.

At the same time that Confucius was striving to mold society into a perfect whole by decisive action and widespread reform, a new school of thought emerged in China. Under the influence of Lao Tse, a shadowy and almost legendary figure of whom very little is known, a group of people reacted against Confucian conformity and sought to establish a natural rhythm of life based on harmony with the universe, tranquillity, and contentment.

Taoism, the result of this quest for freedom of spirit and mind, is divided into two distinct parts—a philosophy and a religion. The first is remarkable for its inner quietness, the second for its outward display.

Taoist philosophy arose from an intellectual revolt by scholarly men against what they considered was artificial and harmful organization. They expressed an instinctive belief that nature should take its inevitable course, and that if people were true to themselves they could not go wrong. There is a strong sense of fatalism in Taoist philosophy, and a feeling that it is fruitless to fight against destiny.

In its outward form, Taoism turned into a mystical religion notable for the enormous number and infinite variety of its gods. It was developed by priest magicians who used magic spells and charms, and conducted rites to preserve man's true self and give him long life. Taoists worshiped gods of the earth and heaven, ancestors and dragons, literature and the kitchen, and almost every imaginable object, event, emotion, or emergency in life. Taoist religion has appealed mainly to the illiterate masses and its influence has recently declined; but Taoist philosophy has had a profound effect on Chinese thinking and culture. Through ideals of true simplicity and infinite quietness it has left its mark on painting and poetry, and on Chinese life.

In 221 B.C., Shih Huang Ti, prince of the Ch'in people, defeated the last Chou warlord and captured his territories. Shih Huang Ti extended his frontiers northward, past the site of the present capital of Peking, and southward to the fertile valley of the Yangtze, the greatest river in Eastern Asia. This new empire was soon known as China, the land of the Ch'in.

This first Ch'in emperor was a ruthless dictator. He collected tribute from vassal kings and chiefs and spent a great deal of it on large armies, imposing palaces, and fine roads. He also completed the Great Wall of China which had been started by his predecessors to keep out barbarian foes. It was a gigantic line of defense, with its turreted watchtowers and strongly fortified gateways stretching for fifteen hundred miles. The Great

Wall repelled all but the most powerful invaders for two thousand years.

When Shih Huang Ti died, the Ch'in dynasty crumbled; but in 202 B.C. the first Han emperor mounted the throne and enlarged his realm. At the time of Christ the Chinese Empire equaled the Roman Empire in size and strength, and traveling merchants carried samples of Chinese art and accounts of her wealth to the Western world. By camel and horse they made the long land journey from the shores of the Yellow Sea to the distant Mediterranean, bearing bales of silk, jade carvings, bronze statues, lacquer ornaments, and pieces of precious porcelain. They visited Egypt, Greece, and Rome, and brought back a variety of goods and stories of strange peoples and unfamiliar gods.

The Han dynasty lasted for more than four hundred years and during this time Buddhism reached China. Tradition recounts how in A.D. 63 the Han emperor Ming-ti dreamed of a golden man flying into his palace by night. The emperor conferred with the court oracles who saw in the vision the coming of an Indian god. Ming-ti was impressed by the omen and sent messengers to India to investigate religion there. They brought back Buddhist images, copies of the scriptures, and monks of the Mahayana school to interpret them to the emperor. The party returned in a vehicle drawn by a white horse, and the first Buddhists to settle in China built the White Horse Monastery, in the northeastern province of Honan, where it still stands today, marking the great significance of the journey.

At first Confucian scholars opposed the new religion. They objected to the rules of Buddhist Orders which forbade monks to marry and interrupted the stream of family life; and they disapproved of men begging for a living instead of earning it. Though Buddhism, Confucianism, and Taoist philosophy shared a love of peace and a desire for truth which gave them a common purpose, it was three hundred years before Mahayana monks overcame Confucian hostility. Then, at last, Buddhism took its place on equal terms beside the established Chinese religions. It has never been possible since that day to count the members of any one faith in China because so many people accept some part of them all. Taoist gods are represented in Buddhist temples and no prudent Chinese of any religion would deny the presence and importance of ancestral spirits.

In the ninth century, Buddhist communities suffered their first outright persecution. By this time a number of Mahayana missionaries had come from India to work in China. They founded monasteries, built temples, some of which they shared with Taoist gods, gained a substantial following, and accumulated considerable wealth. The ruling emperor of the Tang dynasty resented Buddhist power and coveted Buddhist gold. He sacked shrines, seized the monasteries, and drove out the monks.

Buddhism recovered slowly from this wholesale destruction and then had to face renewed repression. The Tang emperors attacked Confucianism and Buddhism in turn, according to their personal convictions. During this period of religious insecurity, Buddhism and Confucianism grew closer together, and a way of religious thought was born of the two faiths, containing elements of both. It was known as Neo-Confucianism and has endured for a thousand years.

Religious belief combined with artistic talent produced in China some of the loveliest buildings in the world. The first Buddhists to arrive constructed their monasteries and temples in the way that they knew best, following the traditional Indian pattern. But gradually Chinese artists imposed their own ideas on the foreign builders in their midst and a new style of architecture came into being. The solid towers of stone and brick gave way to shining, many-storied pagodas, rising like fantastic flowers from city streets, open country, and sacred sites on the tops of mountains. They were designed mainly as bell towers, soaring sheer above the surrounding roofs, though some included at their base a chamber containing holy relics and statuary.

Chinese architecture reached a glorious peak about A.D. 1200, and then, little by little, lost some of its slenderness and brilliance. But many pagodas still exist in dazzling splendor, the tapering roofs patterned with colored tiles, the doors and windows framed with gleaming lacquer, and the tips of the eaves hung with tinkling golden bells.

The precincts of most Buddhist temples in China, and also in Japan, are similar in design. An impressive gateway opens onto a paved cloister where the pagoda and the main hall of the temple stand. Within the hall the Buddha is majestically enshrined. Often his figure is golden, sometimes carved in stone, marble, or jade, and he sits cross-legged on a pedestal or great lotus leaf. Some Buddhas hold one hand outstretched in blessing; others are presented in an attitude of utter repose. Usually they are surrounded by statues of *bodhisattvas* who are

A figure of Guatama Buddha in the Chinese temple of Kuangchi

Buddhist priests in a temple courtyard

deeply revered because in their extreme goodness and humanity thye have given up their place in Nirvana to come to the aid of mankind. Near the main temple building is the hall of law where priests instruct their students in the *sutras,* the Chinese translation of Buddhist scriptures. Beyond the cloister wall are groups of smaller temples, used as dwelling houses by the priests. Once the pattern of temple building was set, it changed little. It is probably true to say that for nearly two thousand years, Buddhism influenced Chinese art and architecture, while Confucianism directed the law and literature.

For dynasty after dynasty China stood in splendid isolation, supreme in Eastern Asia and untroubled by other continents. But from the eighteenth century onward the Chinese position was challenged on all sides: Russia began to take an interest in foreign affairs and claimed recognition as a world power; the United States of America declared its independence; and a hundred years later Japan developed with terrifying speed from a weak backward nation of no international importance to a highly mechanized modern state with violent territorial ambitions. In this world-wide political and scientific activity China was left far behind.

In 1894, war broke out between China and Japan over the possession of the country of Korea, and the mighty Chinese Empire was swiftly and decisively defeated by her much smaller, but far more efficient, neighbor.

In 1912, a boy emperor, the last of the reigning Manchu dynasty, was forced to abdicate the Chinese throne and a revolutionary leader named Sun Yat Sen was elected president of a republic. Two world wars and outright Japanese aggression brought China to the verge of ruin and fresh revolution. In the Second World War, under the leadership of Generalissimo Chiang Kai-shek, she fought with the United States and Britain against Japan, and in 1945 shared in the Allied victory. But by this time a Communist Government held supreme power in the Soviet Union, and Party leaders openly declared their intention of converting the entire world to Communism. Divided and disorganized, China was a fertile field for Communist propaganda. With Soviet aid, Mao Tse-tung, a Chinese Communist, headed a revolt against the Nationalist Government of Chiang Kai-shek. Civil war swept through the country. Chiang Kai-shek was driven from one city after another until he was forced to withdraw to the offshore island of Formosa. On October 1, 1949, Mao Tse-tung triumphantly proclaimed a Chinese People's Republic in Peking.

Even before the Communists set up their regime in China, the people had weakened in their traditional attitude toward their religions. War had split up families, and young people who used to work on the land were beginning to go to the cities to find jobs in shops and factories. Distances are great and traveling expensive, so they lost touch with their parents. They did not reject Confucianism, but the system which had supported it was breaking down. Many Buddhist temples were damaged during the civil war, the monks dispersed, and the colleges closed. By this time the Taoist religion had deteriorated into a collection of old-fashioned superstitions with nothing to offer educated people.

Confucianism and Communism have directly conflicting loyalties. Confucius taught that obedience to parents and fidelity to the family were the most important duties of every man, woman, and child. Communists believe that service to the state and allegiance to the Party should be the highest ideal of every citizen. By mass education and totalitarian control they are molding the nation. There is no real meeting ground between the two ways of life. The Communists have not openly suppressed religion in China, but they have discouraged it. They have organized huge communal farms and distributed monastery lands among landless peasants. They have restored temples and converted some into community centers and others into show places, instead of shrines. But the code of Confucius and the principles of the Buddha have been part of Chinese consciousness for so long that it is too early yet to predict that there will be no place for them under Communist rule.

7 · *The Land of the Rising Sun*

THE JAPANESE PEOPLE had no writing until the fifth century of the Christian era, and their documented history begins far later than that of most Far Eastern countries. The origins of the first settlers have never been firmly established, but it is thought that they came from other parts of Asia several thousand years before Christ. Though the Japanese islands are only separated from the Korean mainland by a hundred miles of sea, the early settlers do not appear to have been troubled by fresh migrations or conquests. They had no share in the expanding splendor of Chinese civilization, and developed a nation of their own with a different language and religion from those of their neighbors.

The religion of ancient Japan was Shinto, the Way of the Gods, and, in a modified form, it is the most prevalent faith in the country today.

Shinto was founded on the belief in a Supreme Sun Goddess who lived in the Plain of High Heaven and gave her personal protection to the inhabitants of the Japanese islands.

According to age-old legend, the first settlers were divided among themselves over the choice of a ruling chief, and were therefore always at war. When the Sun Goddess looked down from heaven she saw the conflict and decided to help the unhappy people. So she sent her grandson, Prince Ninigi-no-Mikoto, to earth to find a peaceful solution, and in the year fixed by general consent as 660 B.C. his grandson, Jimmu Tenno, became the first emperor of a united Japan.

The Japanese have, until very recently, proclaimed that their emperors were descended in direct, unbroken line from Jimmu Tenno, great-great-grandson of the Sun Goddess, and that they all ruled with her divine consent. Each one in turn received national homage both as a celestial being and as the human head of the Japanese race. Shinto worship was based on this nationalistic tradition and the priests fostered the proud belief that, as the Japanese had occupied their islands since prehistoric times without foreign intrusion, they were not only related one to the other but also to their royal rulers, and to the Sun Goddess. Every new generation grew up with the positive assurance that this connection with a superior being was the special birthright of the Japanese people, a unique privilege which set them on a higher plane than the rest of mankind.

The Japanese believed too in countless nature gods, or *kami,* spirits of the moon and stars, mountains and rivers, wind and rain, rocks and trees, fruit and flowers. Country people regarded the great volcanic peak of Mount Fuji with a special wonder and fascination. For countless centuries they were convinced that the mountain arose miraculously from the plain in a single night, crowned with gleaming snow. And they dreaded the days when the volcano came to life and the earth trembled, because it was a sure sign of the anger of the gods.

Shinto priests built shrines to the Sun Goddess and to the many *kami*. Because the Japanese had not discovered the arts of writing, carving, or painting, their early shrines were very simple. A mirror stood behind the altar, facing toward the east to reflect the rays of the rising sun as a tribute to the Goddess; and before the doorway graceful rainbow-shaped bridges often spanned a little stream. The people hoped that the *kami* would cross these bridges on their way to the temples, bringing with them promises of fine harvests, good health, and large families.

Shinto was a humane religion. The Sun Goddess did not demand sacrifices of men or beasts, and the *kami* appeared to be satisfied with humble offerings of flowers, fruit, wine, and rice, or lengths of silk, cotton, and linen, which devout worshipers placed on their shrines.

It was only in the nineteenth century that the Japanese became an industrial nation. Before this new machine age, they were an agricultural people, entirely dependent for a living on their crops and silkworms. They lived close to the land, and their religious festivals were almost all connected with seasonal changes, or joyous occasions when people gave thanks for the blessings and beauties of nature. They still celebrate with offerings and prayers the birth of a new moon, the glory of the cherry blossom, the fall of the first snowflakes, and the completion of the rice harvest.

In Shiogama, in northern Japan, every July the people

Shinto harbor festival at Shiogama

hold a harbor festival in honor of the Shiotsuchioti-No-Kami, who is reputed long ago to have taught them how to obtain salt from sea water. The god is carried through the town in a divine palanquin, or litter, to the harbor where a sacred ship awaits him. Then he sets sail on a ceremonial voyage, followed

A sacred palanquin in procession

by a fleet of smaller boats, and before the sun sets he is reverently carried back to his habitual shrine. There are Japanese festivals for children of all ages, a special one for girls and their dolls, and another to give boys courage and strength.

The teachings of Confucius and Buddha entered the country of Korea in the wake of Chinese imperial armies. In the sixth century of the Christian era, Chinese and Korean priests and scholars crossed the narrow strait that flows between Korea and Japan, carrying their beliefs and culture to the Japanese people. Confucianism had changed very little in the thousand years since the death of its founder, but Mahayana Buddhism had absorbed new learning and gained considerable outward grandeur from its contact with Chinese civilization.

When Buddhism first reached Japan, Shinto priests were suspicious and hostile. But their fears were overruled by members of the imperial court, who were impressed by the ritual and dazzled by the magnificence of the new religion. They invited enlightened Chinese to visit the country and explain the mysteries of Buddhist doctrine. They also summoned expert artists and sculptors to demonstrate their skill. The Japanese soon developed a talent for painting and sculpture and learned to imitate Chinese designs and to adjust them to their own taste.

They had already tried to master Chinese writing, but the characters did not fit Japanese sounds, and it was a long and complicated process building an alphabet for practical use. Though Japanese students went to China to study law, literature, and religion, when they returned home they were handicapped by the difficulty of expressing themselves clearly in their own written language.

Confucianism made its mark in Japan more slowly than Buddhism. It did not at first win the support of the aristocracy who distrusted Confucius' democratic ideas and disregard for noble birth; and as his followers brought no golden images and prescribed no mysterious ritual it failed to attract the mass of ordinary people.

Though Japanese emperors reigned in undisputed succession, they did not establish a permanent capital. Shinto, in common with many other early religions, regarded corpses as unlucky and unclean. So when an emperor died, his heir vacated the residence defiled by death and built himself a new palace. The impact of Chinese culture and the advent of Buddhism changed the outlook on mortality, and Japanese travelers returned from visiting the Chinese court and described the imperial city of Ch'ang-an in glowing terms as a center of beauty, a seat of government, and a symbol of power.

In A.D. 710, Gemmyo, one of the few great Japanese empresses, decreed that a fixed capital should be built at Nara, in Honshu Island, around her imperial palace, on the Chinese model. By this time the Buddhist clergy were extremely powerful. They had amassed great wealth from devout emperors and ambitious nobles. Their monasteries were like castles and their temples outshone the Shinto shrines in majesty and splendor. They even raised private armies to enforce their commands and had moved far away from the compassionate and peaceful aims of the Buddha. In 749, the Great Buddha of Nara was completed. He sits there now, an immense golden figure on a spreading lotus leaf, aloof and mysterious. After the opening ceremony, people told of a miraculous moment when the Buddha opened his eyes and gazed with understanding and tenderness on the assembled company. At the end of the eighth century the court moved to Kyoto, fifty miles distant, to escape Buddhist domination. But the leaders of the Order followed and in beautiful wooded surroundings built temples even richer and more numerous than those at Nara.

By this time Buddhism and Shinto were presenting an outward appearance of unity. Though Shinto was concerned mainly with bodily welfare and Buddhism with spiritual salvation, they did not openly clash. Shinto priests realized that they could not rival Buddhist might so they came to terms with it. In the cities and the towns, Buddhist altars and Shinto shrines shared the same temples and most families worshiped at both. In country districts, the peasants were more old-fashioned and fearful of change. They clung to the simple cult of folk Shinto, putting their trust in the *kami* their ancestors had worshiped before them.

The emperors never lost the spiritual homage of the people, but they were gradually forced out of worldly leadership. In 1192, a military regime was established in Japan which lasted for seven hundred and fifty years. Warlords seized political power and determined not to share it. They created a national image of an imperial sovereign, too sacred to deal with affairs of state or mix with ordinary men. The emperors lived in majestic solitude and reigned without ruling.

While political changes had been taking place in Japan, a new school of religious thought was born in China. Within the framework of Mahayana Buddhism, Ch'an, better known by the Japanese word Zen, came into being. Zen means "meditation." It is a faith of the mind and the spirit, a union between nature and the inmost soul of man. Zen urges its followers to find the answers to the great questions of life within themselves. Those who practice it successfully empty their minds of cluttered untidy thoughts until they are clear, pure, and quiet. Then they are ready to receive the great truths of the universe. Zen seeks perfection in all things. It creates a standard not only in virtue, art, and learning, but also in everyday living, so that simple duties like cooking and gardening take on a new meaning. Zen exerted its greatest influence in China in the seventh and eighth centuries. In Japan today there are several Zen sects, and they play an important part in modern Buddhism.

Tea drinking had long been a feature of Japanese life, and after the coming of Zen, the Tea Ceremony became a recognized rite. At first Zen monks used it to stimulate their minds at times of meditation. Later it was adopted by laymen, people outside the priesthood, as a valuable means of retreat from the cares and pressures of everyday life. Statesmen took advantage of the quiet hours of the Tea Ceremony to escape from the burdens of office and business men from the worries of commerce, as they still do today. It is an opportunity for reflection alone, or in the company of friends, which seldom occurs in a busy life. The ritual is formal but simple, and

Learning the Tea Ceremony

above all, unhurried. In order to create the right atmosphere many Japanese build special rooms for the ceremony and use them for no other purpose. The floors are covered with rush matting, the walls free from ornament except for one alcove containing a single painted scroll or an object of natural beauty, perhaps a piece of rock or a spray of flowers. All the utensils used in the Tea Ceremony are selected with the utmost care to fulfill a particular function. They are not necessarily of great value, but each one is just right for its own purpose. The host prepares the tea himself from finely powdered green leaves. He mixes them in a china bowl with a bamboo whisk into what a Chinese writer described as "the froth of the liquid jade," and serves it with a silver ladle. As the guests sip the tea they talk to each other or remain silent as the spirit moves them. From the friendly communion and the quietness of the Tea Ceremony they emerge relaxed and with renewed strength.

Many Mahayana sects besides those of Zen appeared in Japan and won many converts. The Pure Land Sect, under the Japanese name of Shin, became very popular in the days when the court moved from Nara to Kyoto and has remained so ever since. Shin Buddhism is the strongest sect in Japan today with more temples, teachers, and believers than any other. Many Japanese, in common with many Christians, are attracted to a doctrine which stresses above all the value of unquestioning faith. They feel secure in the assurance of heavenly bliss in return for placing their trust in Amida Buddha.

In 1543, Europeans landed in Japan for the first time. A Chinese ship carrying three Portuguese sailors among its crew was wrecked on the Japanese coast. Local fishermen rescued the stranded men and gave them food. After a while the Portuguese were picked up by a visiting ship and when they reached home they reported on the conditions in Japan and paid tribute to the kindness of these hitherto unknown people. European merchants were beginning to probe Far Eastern markets and they set out to explore the possibilities of trade with Japan. They were closely followed by priests of the newly founded Jesuit Order, zealous in the Christian cause. The Japanese received this new faith with the same interest they had shown to other foreign religions. They studied Christian teaching and found that it did not, in general, conflict with the Buddhist way of life. Many people were converted and baptized, to the intense fury of the Buddhist clergy.

For nearly a hundred years the Jesuits increased their following, and trade between Japan and Europe prospered. But the warlords were hard masters, and in 1637 a band of Japanese Christians led a revolt against gross misrule. The rising was sternly suppressed and all converted Christians were ordered to recant. If they refused they were tortured, killed, or shipped out of the country. Soon afterward the ruling warlord issued a decree banishing every foreigner from the islands. No Japanese were allowed to leave the country, no ship from any other nation was admitted to a Japanese port, and no shipyard was permitted to build a vessel large enough to make an overseas voyage. The only Europeans who remained in Japan were a handful of Dutch traders who were forbidden to hold a religious service. For the next two hundred years Japan had practically no contact with the outside world.

Meanwhile, respect for Confucian teaching had steadily gained ground among educated people. During the long period of isolation it had a profound influence on the governing warlords and set a standard of conduct for the nation as a whole. Discipline was very important in a military regime, and the

Japanese are not by nature a rebellious people. They readily accepted rules of behavior based on an established pattern. Almost as a matter of course they obeyed their parents, gave way to their superiors, and revered their ancestors. A marriage was not a personal affair, but a contract drawn up between two families without consulting the wishes of the boy and girl most deeply involved. In the long run, Confucian conformity was as acceptable to the people and as useful to the government in Japan as it had been in China.

Already in Japan the cult of *bushido* had been adopted by the warrior class. In a curious way, hard for Western people to understand, *bushido* arose from the perfectionist doctrines of Buddhism, particularly Zen Buddhism, applied to the art of war. It was based on belief in the unimportance of living and the ability to stand on the verge of death clear-sighted and unafraid. It probably began as a military code and it grew into something very like a religion. *Bushido* rated obedience and courage above all the other virtues, and weakness as sinful. The greatest honor a peasant soldier could hope for was to lay down his life in battle for his lord. Surrender was shameful and any form of failure a lasting disgrace. Generals encouraged the belief that death was better than dishonor, and their men fought to the death. When they were defeated they committed suicide, or *hara-kiri,* rather than be taken prisoner.

In the middle of the nineteenth century, the Western powers broke into Japanese seclusion. Japan lay directly on the Pacific trade route between the United States and China, and her harbors were valuable for shipping. For a time the Japanese resisted all Western approaches. But finally Commodore Perry of the United States Navy steamed into a harbor very near the present port of Yokohama with seven warships, and refused to leave until a trade treaty was signed. Other nations followed and the Japanese people renewed their relations with the outside world. They soon realized that they were two hundred years behind the West in scientific development and technical skill and swiftly determined to bridge the gap. Within forty years, by painstaking imitation and almost superhuman devotion to duty, they accomplished an industrial miracle.

They also reorganized the government, and in 1868 the principal lords of Japan were summoned to Kyoto to proclaim the restoration of imperial rule. A young emperor, Meiji Tenno, became once more a living emblem of national harmony and a rallying point for every loyal citizen. Religion played a large part in this newly found unity. Ambitious politicians suppressed Buddhism and established Shinto as a state religion. They used it to whip up patriotism and promote national pride, and revived the belief that the Japanese were a master race, destined to rule. This fanatical faith in inevitable superiority and invincible strength led them to think they could do no wrong. In December, 1941, Japanese armed forces attacked the United States' Hawaiian island base of Pearl Harbor, and in the next four years, true to the code of *bushido,* millions of Japanese willingly died to fulfill what they had been taught to regard as a divine mission.

The humiliation of crushing defeat and unconditional surrender in 1945 shattered the foundations of Japanese belief.

The victorious Allied leaders drafted a new constitution for Japan, based on democratic principles and religious freedom. The emperor was allowed to keep his throne on condition that he openly denied his inherited divinity and agreed to serve his people as a human monarch. The Japanese armed forces were disbanded, and State Shinto, with its violent nationalist propaganda, was abolished.

In post-war Japan there is no dominant religion. Shinto, in an earlier form than State Shinto, has been re-established. Mahayana Buddhism with its many sects has regained much of its former greatness, and many Japanese worship at both Shinto and Buddhist shrines. The standard of Buddhist scholarship is very high indeed. Confucianism has retained a number of loyal followers. Less than one per cent of the Japanese people are Christian, but their influence outweighs their numerical strength.

In the grim aftermath of total war, with the shame of surrender and the suffering caused by the two atomic bombs that fell on Japanese cities, many people sought comfort in religion. Hundreds of new religious sects arose to cater for the needs of a defeated but dynamic nation. Almost all these new cults are linked in some way to traditional beliefs, but many direct their efforts towards practical ends, public welfare, and social service. Every new sect trains its own teachers and holds services and meetings that are generally less formal and more friendly than those of the established religions, and about a hundred of them belong to the Union of New Religious Cults.

The new doctrines tend to be simple and easily under-

The High Priest of Shinto

stood by ordinary people. A good example is the Perfect Liberty Corporation which teaches that: (1) every man is the son of God; (2) life is art; (3) the life of man is self-expression;

(4) one must live as brightly as the sun; (5) men are equal; and (6) perfect liberty is the guiding principle of life. It is not difficult to recognize in these ideals the inherited traditions of Shinto, Buddhism, and Confucianism so deeply ingrained in the Japanese character.

8 · *The Greek Way of Life*

IN THE FIFTH and fourth centuries B.C., Greek civilization reached its height and in that age of beauty and learning the people of Greece filled their land and their literature with statues and stories of their gods. Philosophy and poetry, politics and sport, love and war, art and architecture, music and dance, law and reason were all linked to religious belief.

Religion gave to many educated Greeks a high moral standard and an inner strength. To the simple people it was a social life and a source of protection. To all Greeks it was a reason for getting together to do the things they enjoyed most. Poetic contests, dramatic festivals, and above all the athletic games were conducted with immense fervor under the patronage of particular gods and goddesses.

Many scholars now believe that the Greeks, or Hellenes, as they are also called, learned a way of life and a love of beauty from a people who lived in the nearby island of Crete. This Minoan civilization, named after King Minos who ruled in the Cretan capital of Cnossos, was probably almost as old as those of Sumeria and the Indus Valley. Paintings and sculptures show that the Minoans were small and dark like the people of North Africa, but no one knows when they settled in Crete.

As archaeologists uncover fine palaces, graceful pottery, and lifelike statues, the age-old history of the Minoan people is gradually unfolding and their religious beliefs are revealed. Within the palaces and in groves of sacred trees they set up shrines to a goddess, represented in human form, who had as her symbols the horns of a bull, crossed axes, the snake, and the dove. She was first and foremost a protector of households, but also believed to be an earth goddess in close touch with nature. Later, under the name of Hera, she was adopted by the Greeks and, as the wife of Zeus, given an important place among the most honored gods.

The Minoans were apparently a peaceful mercantile people, and, feeling secure in their command of the surrounding seas, they did not trouble to fortify their cities. For many years classical scholars examined Minoan records, trying to discover why the kingdom collapsed and how the civilization spread to Greece. They have recently deciphered an early script which shows that by 1400 B.C., Greek-speaking people had crossed the Aegean Sea in their many-oared ships and settled in Crete. Evidently a war broke out and Cnossos was destroyed, but by this time some Greeks had absorbed Minoan culture and carried it back to the mainland.

Greeks who lived much later called the original inhabitants of the Peloponnese, the land nearest Crete, Pelasgians. In a long series of migrations Greek tribes came down from the north and imposed their language on the Pelasgian population.

The horns of a bull, symbol of the Cretan goddess

Latest and most warlike of all the invaders were the Dorians, who, it is thought, arrived about 1100 B.C. and founded the state of Sparta. But though the Pelasgians lost their language they kept some of their early beliefs. The Athenians who contributed so much to the glory of Greece claimed that they had lived in these parts from the beginning of time, and they wore golden grasshoppers in their hair as a sign of belonging to the ancient earth. It is quite possible that both they and the Ionians who occupied a strip of coast and a chain of islands in Asia Minor came from Pelasgian stock.

Homer, the earliest and the greatest of all the Greek epic poets, was an Ionian. His famous poems, the *Iliad* and the *Odyssey,* were regarded as almost sacred, and his writings, with their mixture of religion and fantasy, had a profound effect on the thinking and morality of the Greek world. Homer probably lived in the eighth century before Christ, and in his day a Hellenic language with various dialects prevailed throughout southern Greece.

By this time Athens had grown into an important center of culture and trade. But though the Hellenic people in general were intensely proud of their achievements, they did not attempt to form a single kingdom. From the age of Homer until they were conquered by Alexander the Great in the fourth century B.C., they successfully resisted political unity. They established independent city-states, or *poleis,* which were the basis of their civilization. A *polis* was a citadel and source of security for its own citizens, who were proud of their independence and considered the city-state a perfect arrangement. Each one had an individual government, and this system created intense patriotism. As all the *poleis* were self-governing and self-supporting, they had no desire to sacrifice their sovereignty for a small share in a great empire. The people of Athens, Sparta, Corinth, Thebes, Ephesus, and many other city-states built their own temples, stadiums, theaters, and market places, made their own laws, raised their own armies, and upheld their

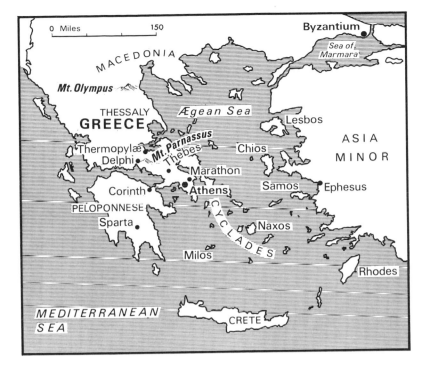

Ancient Greece

own traditions. At first every *polis* had its own gods, but gradually the twelve Olympians, with Zeus at their head, were universally accepted by the Greeks.

Religion in pre-Christian Greece differed in many important aspects from other faiths of that time. In Judaism, Hinduism, and Buddhism the temples were closely guarded and the ritual was laid down by professional clergy who devoted their entire lives to those religious duties. They occupied positions of power and privilege in the community because of their sacred calling and they were usually the most learned people in the land.

The Greeks founded no holy orders and built no monasteries to train men for full-time priesthood. Every Greek citizen was a high priest in his own home, and almost all the temple services were conducted by magistrates and other public figures who were chosen for a particular occasion. Service to the state and bringing up families were honored tasks too, so very few men were required to give them up in order to dedicate their lives to the gods. Each temple was regarded as the house of its own particular god, and sacrifices and ceremonies took place outside the pillared walls, in the open air.

The Greeks did not possess a sacred book like the Torah with inflexible Commandments inspired by one almighty God; nor did they have, like the later Christians, a set creed to regulate their thoughts. Their curiosity and imagination were unbounded and they were always interested in other peoples' ideas and ready to compare them with their own.

Most city-states were composed of three classes: citizens who had full political rights, resident foreigners with limited rights, and slaves who had none at all. The slaves did almost all the manual work so that the freemen had leisure to serve the state. In Athens not only men of noble birth but also traders and craftsmen were full citizens, and took part in public affairs. The government was carried out by well-to-do Athenians who gave their services free and poorer citizens who took public office and were rewarded with a fee. Every freeman had to be prepared, if he were elected, to serve the state at all times. They acted as soldiers, judges, priests, or members of the government as the need arose. They spent their lives in each other's company, meeting in the market place, the Assembly, at athletic gatherings, or the theater. Educated Athenians did not specialize in a single art or profession. They studied literature, mathematics, music, law, philosophy, statecraft, and military tactics. They talked endlessly about everything for they were passionately eager to learn.

Greek civilization was never undermined by easy wealth and luxurious living, for Greece is a poor country. A thin layer of soil covers the rocky ground and life has always been a struggle. Wheat, olives, and grapes were the main crops. From earliest times the olive tree provided many necessities of Greek life: food for the people, fuel for their fires and lamps, oil to anoint those who served the gods, and branches to crown the victors at the Olympic games.

Women took no part in public life. They stayed at home and carried out their household duties, and the main purpose of every marriage was to produce children.

In peace and war, sorrow and happiness, sickness and health, the Greeks looked toward Mount Olympus, the dwelling place of their chief gods and goddesses. It lies in northern Greece, a massive snow-capped peak, frequently wreathed in mist and always filled with mystery. Its summit seemed to humble humans to be far nearer heaven than earth.

The twelve Olympian deities were considered powerful but far from perfect. They had faults and failings like human beings. They were often jealous and sometimes cruel, lost their tempers, and committed foolish mistakes. They fell in love, went to war, and experienced pleasure and pain. Through poetry and drama

Mount Olympus, the throne of Zeus

the legend of their lives was woven into the history of every city-state. People criticized their conduct and questioned their judgment, but at the same time erected glorious temples in their honor.

Each of the Olympian gods and goddesses had his or her especial realm. Zeus was mightiest of them all, god of the sky, wielder of thunderbolts and master of lightning, controller of the weather, and lord of all he surveyed. The Greeks believed that from his exalted position Zeus saw everything that happened on earth, so his realm was boundless and his power unlimited.

Zeus was married to Hera, the ancient Minoan goddess who had been brought from Crete to make her home in Greece. She became guardian of marriage and the home, watched over childbirth and recognized family needs. She was a practical and motherly goddess and the people loved her.

Pindar, the Greek lyric poet, relates in the sixth century B.C. how the goddess Athene was born from the brain of Zeus and came out of his head. She was wise, beautiful, skilled in household crafts, and even experienced in affairs of state. High on the Acropolis, Athenians built the Parthenon, an exquisite temple of white marble, and dedicated it to Athene.

Apollo, one of the many sons of Zeus, represented everything that the Greeks admired most. He was an example of perfect manhood, a fine athlete, an accomplished musician, and an upholder of law and order. Poets tell how he conquered Delphi and built a temple where an oracle, inspired by the divine wisdom of Apollo, made prophecies for the good of the Greek people. According to Greek legend, Zeus had decided to

The temple of Apollo at Delphi

discover the exact center of the earth by releasing two eagles from opposite ends of the world and watching their course. They flew toward each other and met over Delphi, proving that this was the central point.

The ruins of the temple of Apollo lie high in the mountain range of Mount Parnassus, on a shelf of pearl-gray rock with sheer cliffs above and a steep drop to the valley hundreds of feet below. Men who made pilgrimages to consult the oracle must have felt that they were climbing very close to the gods.

There are varying reports of the Delphic ritual and it undoubtedly changed from one century to the next. But most historians agree that in an inner sanctuary of the temple the Pythia, a mortal woman chosen to be the priestess and mouthpiece of Apollo, sat on a golden tripod attended by a band of priests. At appointed times the Pythia prepared to receive inquiries and made oracular responses which everyone accepted as the words of Apollo.

The regular time for consultation was the seventh day of the month, except for the three midwinter months when the oracle did not speak. Shortly after dawn, the priests poured cold water over a goat in order to find out if the day was a lucky one. If the goat shivered, it was counted a good omen. They then sacrificed the goat outside the temple, to announce to the waiting people that the ceremony was about to begin. If the goat did not react to the icy shower, the consultations were postponed.

The Delphic oracle was greatly in demand. Kings and statesmen came from all the Mediterranean countries to seek counsel from Apollo on matters of state. They inquired whether it was advisable to found new colonies, and they approached the oracle before going to war or financing a new enterprise. Ordinary people brought their personal problems, asking if they should get married, what profession they should choose, and which crops they should plant. The inquirers presented their questions to the priests. They in turn passed them on to the Pythia, who fell into a trance before she was able to pronounce the answers.

Delphic prophecies were often sound and far-seeing, for the keepers of the shrine recruited a force of messengers, who operated rather like a news service. They traveled far and wide, bringing back the latest information from every Mediterranean shore for Greek guidance. Hence the oracle gained a reputation for exceptional vision, and Delphi grew rich on the fees and gifts which people gave in return for the consultations.

Hermes, the swift and trusted messenger of the gods, was also a son of Zeus. Hermes controlled fertility, and people sacrificed animals on the altars before his temples, praying that he would give them fine children and their farm livestock plentiful offspring. Many Greeks erected a rough-hewn pillar, shaped like a naked man, outside their homes as a tribute to Hermes and a token of good luck.

Poseidon was god of the sea, of rivers and lakes, streams and springs, and also the god of earthquakes. His symbol was a three-pronged spear, and when he struck the earth water gushed forth. Sailors and fishermen laid thank offerings on his altars and sang his praises when they came safely to port.

The Greek delight in beauty found its expression in the goddess Aphrodite. She was the goddess of love and of loveliness, symbolic of romance and feminine charm. Sculptors made countless statues of her, naked or in clinging robes. Poets composed glowing versions of her birth, and the most romantic of them all depicts her rising radiantly from the ocean, her skin gleaming like rose-tinted marble and her hair as soft as silk.

One of the most interesting Olympians was Hephaistos, the craftsman of the gods, skilled in arts and divinely qualified to manufacture weapons and armor, crowns and jewelry, furniture and chariots, and whatever else the gods needed. Hephaistos was lame and awkward but very clever, and there was no limit to his inventiveness.

Ares was the Olympian god of war. He was not as popular as the other gods because he was associated with death and destruction, and most Greeks regarded war in itself as wasteful and fruitless. But the citizens of every city-state knew they had to fight for their independence, and they never went to war without first seeking Ares' divine protection.

Artemis was the goddess of hunters. Her domain covered the woodlands and the rivers; she was queen of the trees and wild plants; and the beasts, birds, and fishes were her subjects.

Demeter, goddess of fields and crops, produced the corn and fruit on which life depended. She was greatly beloved by the country people and her temples were decked with garlands of flowers. There is a beautiful Greek hymn to Demeter which tells us how her daughter Persephone was stolen by Hades, god of the underworld. Demeter grieved so sadly for her lost daughter that she neglected the earth and nothing would grow. The people were dying of starvation and the world was doomed. Finally Zeus sent Hermes to the underworld, and he succeeded in persuading Hades to send Persephone back to her mother for two-thirds of the year. During this time Demeter was happy and the earth fruitful, but for the remaining four months the land was bleak and barren. Each spring Persephone returned, the fields flowered once more, and the Greeks marveled and rejoiced.

The last comer to Mount Olympus was Dionysus, god of

the living things of the earth and especially of grapes and wine. He displaced Hestia, goddess of the hearth, but she kept her place in the hearts of the people. Every city and every home had a hearth where a sacred fire burned night and day. If the fire went out it was difficult to rekindle, and Hestia had the important task of keeping them all alight. When the other gods and goddesses went their various way, she stayed at home on Mount Olympus. The Greeks knew that she was attending to her essential duties and were content.

The festivals of Dionysus were celebrated with mystic rites of animal sacrifice, dance, and song. People feasted with wine and experienced wild ecstasy, uplifted by the feeling that they were temporarily blessed with divine power and granted a glimpse of immortality.

The athletic games were the most notable event in the Greek calendar. There were four great festivals—at Delphi, the Isthmus of Corinth, Nemea in the Peloponnese, and Olympia. The Olympic games, which have become the most famous, began in the eighth century B.C. and they became increasingly popular. The games were combined with religious ceremonies and carried out with precision and pageantry. Every four years heralds proclaimed a sacred truce throughout the Greek world, and athletes gathered from all the city-states and from Greek colonies in Africa, Asia, and Italy to compete. They raced merely for the honor and glory of winning, and the highest award was a simple olive branch. Kings and commoners raced side by side, and the winners became national heroes. Poets and musicians sang their praises and sculptors carved their likeness in gleaming marble. At first the athletes wore loincloths, but one young runner threw his off and won his race. From this time onward men raced without clothes. Nakedness had no shame for the Greeks. They admired the human body and saw no reason to disguise it.

At the beginning of the fifth century B.C., the Persians were the strongest people in Western Asia. They had already conquered Judea and the surrounding countries, and were closing in on Greece. In the face of mortal danger Athens and Sparta overcame their traditional rivalry, formed a league with other city-states, and fought together to repel the invading host. On the plains of Marathon in 490 B.C. the Athenians defeated a vastly superior Persian force. Ten years later Spartan soldiers proved their valor and won everlasting fame at Thermopylae, where a little force of three hundred men held a pass against the mighty Persian army until every single Spartan was killed. In the same year, in the narrow Straits of Salamis, by skill and cunning, the Athenian fleet won a resounding victory over a Persian fleet more than three times its size. But Persian power was not broken and the war continued until in 448 Pericles, the famous Athenian statesman and warrior, succeeded in making a treaty that was favorable to the Greeks.

Pericles was a lawgiver and patron of the arts. He was elected leader of the Assembly, the Athenian parliament, many times, and despite the demands of the war Athens prospered. Soon after the death of Pericles Greek philosophy, literature, and art reached its most glorious peak. In a great wave of genius the people of widely scattered city-states created temples and statues of matchless beauty, wrote poems and dramas of enduring excellence, studied the principles of law and learning, and explored the realms of reason and religion. It was an age of enlightenment which shed its brilliance far beyond the boundaries of Greece, and centuries later was reflected in European culture and thought.

Side by side with the official religion of the city-states and the prescribed worship of accepted gods, there existed a number of mystery religions by means of which certain Greeks tried to discover the nature and ultimate fate of the human soul and explore the prospects of an after-life. The most important of these mystery cults originated at the ancient city of Eleusis close to Athens. The people of Eleusis glorified the goddess Demeter in the belief that she could bestow not only plenty in this life but immortality in the next. Whereas the state religion was designed to protect the city, group, or family as a whole, and to promote social welfare, the mysteries were the outcome of personal needs and individual inquiry into the meaning of life and death. The rites and ritual led up to a final enlightenment, or beholding, so sacred that no outsider has ever discovered how it came about. In the fifth century B.C., Athens conquered Eleusis and took over religious control of the mystery cults. From this time onward, in the hands of men of learning and vision, the mysteries had a profound influence on Greek thought and religious belief.

Outstanding Athenian dramatists like Aeschylus, Sophocles, and Euripides, each in his own way, examined traditional religion. These writers began to condemn bad behavior in the gods just as they would have condemned it in their fellow men. In poetry and drama which has never been surpassed, they recorded their convictions, and for many of their readers a new conception of Zeus slowly matured until he became an ideal and invincible power, acting with perpetual justice and reason, the forerunner of a universal God.

This was an age of great men. In 470 B.C., Socrates was born. Like most other Athenian thinkers, he was a fervent patriot and fought bravely in the wars. The rest of his life he devoted to the pursuit of truth and goodness. He questioned whether the science and philosophy of his time were really in touch with the course of human life. Socrates held that the first step to wisdom was to measure one's own ignorance, and he had a zest for learning and an appetite for knowledge which he was never able to satisfy. He gave up ordinary everyday comforts, wore the simplest garments, and walked barefoot. He talked to both young and old, in the streets and the market place, always asking questions and sifting the answers, seeking a definition of absolute goodness. He must eventually have found some personal solution, but he was too modest to lay down the law for others.

Because Socrates refused to accept as undisputed fact the traditional beliefs of his time, he made many enemies. They accused him of corrupting the young with doubts about state religion and destroying their patriotism. When after a long war Athens was defeated by Sparta, many of the citizens blamed Socrates. At the age of seventy he was tried by an Athenian jury and found guilty of spreading treacherous ideas. The aged philosopher deliberately chose death rather than exile, calmly accepted a cup of poison hemlock, and died serenely, seeking to the end an explanation of the universe and a cure for the ills of mankind. He was one of the very rare Greek martyrs, for freedom of mind was a treasured right.

Socrates himself wrote nothing down. He delivered his teaching by word of mouth and it was preserved and developed by Plato, his devoted friend and pupil, who became the greatest of all the Athenian philosophers. In 387 B.C., twelve years after Socrates' death, Plato founded a university and established there a school of thought which has influenced the civilized world for over one thousand years. He, like Socrates, sought universal perfection, through individual goodness. In his famous book, *The Republic,* he pictured the birth of an ideal state where a few men of outstanding virtue were chosen as natural leaders and educated to rule the rest. Plato was deeply concerned with righteousness, and he reverenced wisdom, honesty, and courage. He taught that the best kind of love is that of purity and excellence, and to him, as to many devout Greeks, politics, philosophy, and religion were one and the same thing. Centuries earlier, Homer had regarded the soul without the body as a poor weak thing fleeing at death "like a twittering bat" to a miserable half-life in Hades. Plato had moved far from this traditional dread of death. He had inherited from the mystery religions high hopes of a future existence, and he valued the soul, which he felt was immortal, far more highly than the body. He developed a doctrine of immortality with a reward for virtue and punishment for evil which had a profound effect on Christian teaching.

While learned men in Greece were probing the relations between God, the universe, and men, power changed hands in

Western Asia. King Philip of Macedonia defeated the city-states of Athens and Thebes and formed an alliance against the emperor of Persia. Impressed with Greek culture, Philip summoned Aristotle, an eminent scientist and philosopher, and former student at Plato's Academy, to instruct his son Alexander. Aristotle studied the habits of the body and the workings of the mind. His findings, like those of Plato, had considerable effect on the development of European thought and the study of science and biology. He instilled into his young pupil a thirst for knowledge which Alexander never lost. He came to the throne when he was twenty, and soon proved himself the greatest soldier of his day. In thirteen years he built an empire which stretched from Greece to the Himalayas and won for himself the title Alexander the Great. He conquered by force of arms, but he ruled with tolerance according to Greek tradition and allowed people to worship the gods who gave them the greatest comfort.

But in Greece itself the foundations of life had crumbled. For the first time, the city-states were forcibly united in a single empire; their separate powers declined and the citizens lost their civic pride and sense of security. They were no longer members of a disciplined society and they had to find a different and more personal way of life.

In Athens, about 300 B.C., a new school of thought was established by Greeks who called themselves the Stoics and their doctrine Stoicism. Though it developed in Greece, Stoicism was a combination of Eastern and Western thought expressed by scholars and priests who gathered in Athens from the far corners of a great empire. The Stoics saw God everywhere, relating the mind and conscience of man to the divine universal mind, in much the same way as some Hindus related the soul of man to the World-Soul (Atman). The Stoics did not deny that God was one with Zeus, but they were anxious to discard once and for all the myths and images and other primitive signs of traditional state religion.

In the second century B.C., Rome won supreme power in the Mediterranean world. Roman legions invaded Egypt, Greece, and Western Asia, and Roman governors took over much of the empire of Alexander the Great. But though they ruled according to Roman law, they did not try to crush the Greek spirit. The vision of Greek philosophers was not dimmed and Stoicism spread, even to Rome itself. Athens, Alexandria, and many other cities maintained their high standard of learning. Prominent among them was the city of Tarsus. There, early in the Christian era, a son was born to a Jewish family who had come from Jerusalem. This boy, named Saul and later renowned as Paul of Tarsus, was brought up most strictly in the Jewish faith. At the same time he spoke Greek and gained an understanding of Greek ideals, a knowledge which probably had a lasting effect on his conduct in later life. When he grew up, he was converted to Christianity and traveled through the Mediterranean countries, passionately proclaiming his new faith. No one man played a greater part in shaping the Christian religion. Paul carried from the tiny state of Judea to the outside world a faith based on the teaching of Christ, the Commandments of Moses, and the wisdom and high ideals of the Greeks.

9 · The Early Christian Church

NEARLY TWO THOUSAND years ago, a son was born to a Jewish family in Judea. This child was named Jesus, and he is worshiped today by nearly a billion Christians, a third of the population of the earth, as the Son of God and the founder of their faith.

People of other religions do not acknowledge that Jesus, later called Christ or the Chosen One, was divine; but they respect him as a man who devoted his life to the pursuit of purity and the good of his fellow men. In the same way that Christians respect the wisdom of Confucius and the teaching of Buddha, their followers admire the work of Jesus Christ.

Almost the only original information about the life of Christ is contained in the second part of the Bible, known as the New Testament. It is set down in the Gospels of the four evangelists—Matthew, Mark, Luke, and John—and the letters of Paul of Tarsus, and they do not always agree, for each writer gives his personal impression of the Master. Students of the Bible have found it difficult to put an exact date to the Gospels, but it is very probable that they were not actually written until some years after the death of Christ. It is quite certain that all four men held him in deepest reverence, and they have presented his teaching with such sincerity and force that people of every race and tongue have been inspired ever since by the sense of his holiness and undying love.

Jesus was Jewish both by nationality and upbringing. Mary, his mother, married a carpenter named Joseph, and they lived very simply in the little town of Nazareth, seventy miles north of Jerusalem. According to the Gospels of Matthew and Luke, God sent down his Holy Spirit to the Virgin Mary. Through this spiritual visitation she conceived a child who an angel of God told her was destined to be the savior of mankind. The Gospel narratives tell how the baby was born in Bethlehem where Mary and Joseph had gone to pay taxes levied by the Roman governor, and how that night a star of matchless brilliance shone down from Heaven, heralding the great event. In those days the birth of noble men was often associated with supernatural signs, so the early Christians readily accepted the star of Bethlehem as a proof of Jesus' majesty and the miracle of his divine origin is woven deeply into the Christian creed.

The authors of the four Gospels were like painters producing individual portraits of the same person. They all wrote in Greek, the common language of the Mediterranean world, and both Matthew and Mark portrayed Jesus as the promised Messiah for whom the Jews had been waiting. John's Gospel was evidently written later and was the outcome of deep reflection on the meaning of Christ's life and teaching. Luke, referred to by Paul of Tarsus as a physician, was the most accomplished writer of the four. He was a Greek and eager to convince the ruling Romans of the truth of Christ. His Gospel has been described as "the most beautiful book" of all time. In the words of Luke, the Christmas story is told to Christian children every year at Christmastide. They know of the infant Jesus lying in a stable among the donkeys and cows because there was no room at the Bethlehem inn; of the shepherds minding their flocks at night, dazzled by the wondrous radiance of the star; and of the heavenly host of angels crying, "Glory to God in the highest, and on earth peace, goodwill toward men."

Luke tells too the very human story of the twelve-year-old Jesus, traveling from Nazareth to Jerusalem with his family to take part in the yearly feast of the Passover, and being fascinated by what he found in the Holy City. When the celebrations ended, Joseph and Mary left with other Jewish families to return to their homes. They were well on the way before they discovered that Jesus was not with them. Mary and Joseph were very worried and turned back to Jerusalem to look for him. After three days' anxious quest, they found the boy in the Temple, utterly absorbed, listening to the rabbis' teaching and asking them searching questions. When Jesus' parents scolded him he did not make excuses. He was simply surprised that they had not known that he was perfectly safe and finding out what God wanted him to do.

Jesus went to school at Nazareth with boys of his own age. He learned to obey the Laws of Moses and to revere the Torah. But as he grew up, he was troubled. It seemed to him that Jewish teachers of his time set so much stress on formal ritual that the message of God had lost its true meaning.

When Jesus was nearing thirty, he heard that his cousin, known throughout Galilee as John the Baptist, was urging people to confess their wrongdoing and come closer to God. John baptized in the River Jordan those who were truly repentant, a rite symbolic of the washing away of sin. Jesus sought out this preacher whose message proved to be so similar to his own later teaching, and was himself baptized. Then Jesus went out into the wilderness to meditate by a mountain now known as the Mount of Temptation. After forty days he returned, secure in the knowledge that he had been chosen by God to save the world.

Jesus' ministry began at this time. For the remaining years of his life he preached earnestly of love and purity, humility and justice, as means of salvation. He was resolved to bring first of all the Jewish people, and then the whole of mankind, together in a brotherhood of faith in God. In the Sermon on the Mount, delivered to a great multitude, Jesus spoke of those who were blessed in the eyes of God: the meek and merciful, the poor and persecuted. And he taught the people a prayer, which begins, "Our Father which art in Heaven." This prayer became known as *The Lord's Prayer,* and it is repeated at almost every Christian service today.

Jesus soon won a reputation as a teacher, a reformer, and a worker of miracles. People came to him for guidance, help, and healing. The authors of the Gospels recount with awe how he raised the dead, gave cripples strength to walk, cast out evil spirits, and fed a hungry throng with five loaves and two small fishes.

The Mount of Temptation

He chose as his intimate companions twelve disciples who went everywhere with him. They were all working men who were locally employed or had been earning their living in simple country trades. Peter, the leader of the twelve, and two other disciples, James and John, were fishermen. When Jesus called them, they left their nets and followed him, marveling at his goodness, wisdom, and miraculous deeds. He spoke to them sometimes in parables, illustrating his meaning with examples from everyday life. But always he stressed the need for universal love: of God for man, of man for God, and of man for man.

Jesus did not seek the support of wealthy and influential citizens. He felt that his mission lay among poor people who were troubled and sick, and outcasts who were frightened because they had done wrong in the eyes of the Lord and the law. He comforted them with the promise that true repentance and perfect faith would wipe out their sins and give them new life.

As Jesus' fame spread, people flocked to hear him. But when his followers hailed him as an earthly Messiah, successor to King David, sent to restore the glory of Israel, Jesus denied it. He told them that he was not concerned with a worldly crown, but only with the invisible kingdom of Heaven which existed in the mind and the spirit of man.

It is evident that Jesus foresaw his martyrdom and made no effort to escape it. Well aware of the danger of angering the high priests, he went to Jerusalem fearlessly making known the ways of God. He lamented the hypocrisy and false pride that had crept into Judaism and counted true faith far more precious than rank or riches. He told the people that all men were equal in the sight of God. The high priests were afraid that Jesus would undermine their authority so they set out to contradict his teaching, pronounced his words blasphemous and his miracles the work of an evil presence referred to in the Jewish scriptures as the devil.

When Jesus' ministry had lasted for three years, he knew that the time had come for him to die. The week of the Passover was approaching and Jesus went to Jerusalem to celebrate the great Jewish feast and to await God's will. He invited his disciples to share with him the traditional banquet on the eve of the Passover. This was their last supper together, and after Jesus' death the breaking of bread and drinking of wine became the most holy sacrament of the Christian Church, the Holy Eucharist or Communion.

When the meal was over, Jesus went to the Garden of Gethsemane on the outskirts of Jerusalem to pray. Toward dawn a crowd of armed men came to the garden, led by the traitorous disciple, Judas Iscariot, who was in the pay of the high priests. Jesus stood trial, and the high priests found him guilty of blasphemy, accused him of treachery against the state, and condemned him to die. But they did not have the authority to carry out the sentence and handed Jesus over to Pontius Pilate, the Roman governor of Judea, telling him that Jesus had preached revolt against Roman rule.

Pilate was not convinced that the prisoner was guilty of political plotting and tried to save his life. But Jesus steadfastly refused to deny that he had been sent by God to lead the Jewish people into the paths of righteousness. Then Pilate offered to

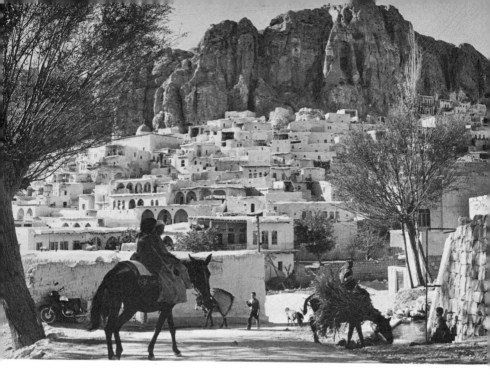

A typical village of the time of Christ

release Jesus according to the custom at Passover, and punish instead a robber named Barabbas. But, spurred on by the high priests, the crowd shouted, "Crucify him, crucify him!" and granted no reprieve. So Jesus was committed to death upon the Cross, an agonizing ordeal usually reserved for the lowest criminals.

At first Jesus' grief-stricken followers saw in his death the contradiction of all his teaching. But they soon realized that the Crucifixion was its supreme fulfillment and that his work had only just begun. When, in deepest mourning, they visited his tomb they were astonished to find it empty. The Gospels relate how on the third day Jesus Christ rose from the dead and afterward revealed himself to his disciples, urging them to carry on his work. They did so willingly, rejoicing in the firm belief that their Master was no longer dead but present with them in a real though invisible manner. They spoke of him being both with God the Father and also present within the Christian community. They used the words "Holy Spirit" to describe Jesus' presence on earth, and the word "Son" to describe his presence with God. So when Christians worship one God they see in him a Holy Trinity of Father, Son, and Holy Spirit, reigning supreme in the kingdom of Heaven where they hope one day to enter.

News of Christ's Resurrection from the dead spread quickly. Headed by Peter, the disciple who had known Christ best, a band of devout Christians set out to carry on his work. When the leaders of the Temple saw that Christianity had survived the death of its founder, they were very angry and determined to destroy the following of Christ. Among the Christians was a man named Stephen, bold in his beliefs. Accused of blasphemy, he refused to recant and was stoned to death. One of the spectators at this gruesome scene was Saul, later Paul, of Tarsus, at that time a firm believer in orthodox Judaism and a declared enemy of Christianity.

After the martyrdom of Stephen, Saul left Jerusalem with orders to track down Christians in Damascus and bring them to trial. On the way Christ spoke to Saul from a cloud of blinding light. This revelation transformed Saul's life and gave the early

Christian Church its greatest missionary leader. He changed his name from the Hebrew Saul to the Greek Paul, and from the day of his conversion became a slave of Christ, utterly dedicated to his service. For the next twenty years, Paul traveled through Palestine, Syria, the countries of Asia Minor that are now Turkey, the cities of Greece, and on to Sicily and Rome, spreading the gospel with burning zeal. Always he delivered a message of hope, preaching that Christ died to save sinners.

Paul was of Jewish stock and educated in Hebrew tradition. He acquired knowledge of Greek ways from living in Tarsus and, in common with the rest of his family, he had been granted Roman citizenship. He was therefore well equipped to carry his message to many different kinds of people in a language and manner that was familiar to them. Sometimes they rose against him, and twice he was almost beaten to death. But he was undaunted by danger and willingly endured pain that would have broken the spirit of men of lesser faith.

Wherever Paul went, he first approached the members of the Jewish community, offering them the gospel or Christian message. If they refused it, and many did, he turned to the Gentiles, people who were not Jews, and made a host of converts. In every town and city he established little Christian churches and, by a ceremony called the "laying-on of hands," ordained elders, later called bishops, to officiate in them. In due course he returned to each community, confirming the people in their faith.

Though the missionary work of Paul of Tarsus and of the disciple Peter is mentioned in the books of the New Testament, their deaths are not recorded. But there is a strong tradition that they preached in Rome and died there in defense of their faith. Christians canonized them both, calling them saints in recognition of their holiness, and enshrined their bones. Through the martyrdom of St. Peter and St. Paul, Rome became especially sacred, and the Bishop of Rome more important than all other Christian clergy.

During the life of Jesus, Christianity was simply a small sect of Judaism and all his followers were Jewish. They had been brought up according to the words of the Torah, many of which were identical with the teaching of Christ, so they had no reason to change their way of life. On the other hand, the Gentiles who became Christians broke away from their ancient traditions. They gave up pagan gods for a faith which held high hopes of immortality, but they refused to enter the Christian Church by way of Judaism, and they rejected circumcision as a foreign custom. These Gentiles acknowledged the divinity of Christ, whereas devout Jews, schooled to steadfast belief in the one God of Israel, could not tolerate any division of divine power. Differences such as these prepared the way for a final break between Judaism and Christianity.

In the year A.D. 70, it came. The Orthodox Jews in Jerusalem planned a rebellion against Roman rule, and the Christians, clinging to Jesus' love of peace, refused to support them. As the day of the uprising drew near, Christian Jews left the city, crossed the River Jordan, and settled in a town named Pella. The Romans suppressed the revolt with atrocious severity, destroyed the Temple, and massacred thousands of Jews. The survivors were banished from Jerusalem and they never forgave the Christians for their desertion.

During the boyhood of Christ, in the reign of the Emperor Augustus, the Roman Empire had reached the peak of its power. In two hundred years the city of Rome had grown from a small republic to the capital of a vast realm. The emperors ruled over Spain, Gaul (the present France), Italy, the northern coast of Africa, Palestine, Egypt, Syria, and part of Asia Minor. Paved roads fanned out like giant spokes from Rome to subject states in Europe and Asia, and the Mediterranean Sea was a Roman lake. Lands within the Empire were free from war and the seas were swept clear of pirates. Roman citizens took prosperity for granted. Roman law prevailed in many lands, Roman legions patrolled the frontiers, and Latin took its place beside Greek as the language of educated people throughout the Empire.

Each new conquest had brought fresh wealth and new forms of worship to the imperial city. Scholars gathered from the far-flung provinces of the Empire, merchants brought their choicest wares, and victorious legions returned with foreign captives who refused to abandon their native gods. Temples of the Egyptian goddess Isis and the Persian god Mithra stood beside the shrines of Roman deities. Many Roman gods and goddesses resembled the Greek Olympians: Jupiter, mightiest of them all, was akin to Zeus; Mars, the Roman god of war, was not far removed from Ares; and whereas in Athens Hestia had tended an eternal flame, in Rome the attendant virgins of the goddess Vesta kept a sacred fire alight.

So when the first Christians arrived, the Romans regarded

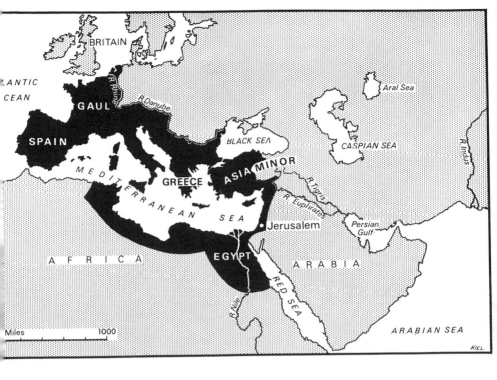

The Roman Empire at the time of St. Paul

them as unimportant disciples of yet another foreign faith and
took little notice of them. But it was not long before Christian
conduct and discipline impressed the leading citizens of Rome.
Successive emperors and members of the senate observed, at first
with respect, and then with fear, the growing strength and resolution of the early Christians, and eventually determined to destroy
them.

These followers of Christ were known as Nazarenes. In
times of persecution they were flogged, stoned, and thrown into

the Roman arenas to be devoured by lions. But it seemed they possessed an inner peace which defied suffering. Pagan oppression merely strengthened their faith and drew them closer together, and despite all opposition the Christian Church developed into an organized body.

In the third century, Roman security was shaken by waves of invasion by Germanic tribes pouring into Europe from the north and east. These fierce, fair-haired barbarians, the Goths, Franks, Vandals, Saxons, and many others, came with their families from barren lands, seeking better living in the fertile south. The Romans had grown soft with two hundred years of easy wealth and luxurious living. Vice and corruption had crept into the highest ranks of government. Many statesmen were no longer upright and just, and many soldiers no longer willing to die for the honor of Rome. It was difficult to raise armies to withstand the savage invaders. The external dangers were intensified by internal strife and the Empire weakened by a series of civil wars over the disputed succession to the imperial throne.

In A.D. 300, a Roman general named Constantine, later called The Great, was proclaimed emperor by the legionaries under his command. A historian of that time recounts how, on the eve of an important battle, Constantine saw a fiery cross in the sky. He accepted this vision as an omen of good fortune, emblazoned the Christian emblem on his banner, and directed his soldiers to carry it on their shields. With the Cross before them they went from victory to victory. Constantine was the first Roman emperor to adopt Christianity and he established his new faith throughout his widening realm.

In 313, by the Edict of Milan, Constantine granted freedom of worship to the Christians in the Roman Empire. Soon afterward he went further and made large grants of money to compensate for their losses and suffering through the persecution of former emperors. Later in his reign he declared Christianity the official state religion. Until this time most Christians had been people of humble birth: working men and women, small traders, peasants, and slaves. Suddenly the Christian Church came into public favor and members of every grade of society flocked to join it.

In 324, after a hard-fought struggle, Constantine defeated his last rival for the imperial throne and extended his rule over the eastern provinces of the Empire. When his triumph was complete, he decided to exalt Christianity and make his own name immortal by building a new capital, Constantinople, far from the political problems and pagan practices of Rome. He chose a commanding position on the shores of the Bosporus, at the entrance to the Black Sea, where the ancient Greek city of Byzantium had stood for many years.

Once Constantine made up his mind he wasted no time in carrying out his majestic plan. He summoned the best architects, painters, and craftsmen he could find, and collected materials from all over the Empire. Christian churches, imperial palaces, and public buildings combined the finest architectural forms of East and West, and the treasures of the Orient added brilliance to European designs. In six years Constantinople was completed, surpassing Rome in richness and splendor.

While Constantine planned a new center of Christendom,

disputes arose within the Church over the relationship of Christ to God. Arius, an Alexandrian monk, contested the conception of the Holy Trinity of Father, Son, and Holy Spirit, and maintained that only God was truly divine. He won many followers, particularly in the eastern Greek-speaking parts of the Empire. Constantine was worried by the religious conflict, fearing that it would endanger Christian unity. In 325, he called a council at Nicaea in Asia Minor to consider the question of the Trinity and make a pronouncement. It was the first ecumenical, or universal, Church council, and an epoch-making event in the history of Christianity. Two hundred and fifty bishops gathered at the emperor's bidding, living proof of the growing strength of an organized Church.

Foremost among the defenders of the Holy Trinity was a young priest who later became Bishop of Alexandria and was canonized as St. Athanasius. He was a man of saintly character with a discerning mind; one of a succession of Christian teachers who recognized the mounting influence of Greek culture on European thought and consequently on the Christian Church. Athanasius realized that as Christianity moved out of Palestine into the Greek and Roman worlds, its early beliefs would be confronted by a host of new ideas. He saw that this challenge was too important to be lightly brushed aside and resolved to meet it with judgment and understanding. When the discussions ended, a majority of the Council upheld the divinity of Christ, and Arius and his supporters were defeated. Before the bishops dispersed, they composed the Nicene Creed, the recognized statement of belief of almost all Christian Churches today. It was a sign of the growing strength of Eastern Christianity that in its original form the Nicene Creed was written in Hebrew, the traditional language of the Bible, and also in Greek.

In 330 Constantinople was dedicated to Christianity, and seven years later, shortly before he died, Constantine was publicly baptized. But despite his immense achievements, he fell short of his final goal. He had intended to promote Christianity and succeeded in doing so; but he also intended to unite Christians from all parts of the Empire, and in this he failed. By building Constantinople he split the Christian Church in two. The Christians in the West worshiped in Latin, and maintained that Rome was the center of Christendom. The Christians in the East worshiped in Greek, and paid homage to the Patriarch of Constantinople as an independent leader and the presiding head of their churches.

Constantinople became the capital of the Byzantine Empire, named after the old Greek city of Byzantium. Emperors ruled there for eleven hundred years and levied tribute from many of the territories which had formerly given their allegiance to Rome. With the death of Constantine Europe entered into an age of violence and bloodshed; but the Byzantine emperors maintained a large Christian Empire in Asia and North Africa until the prophet Mohammed founded a new faith in Arabia and embarked on a campaign of religious conquest.

10 · *The Empire of Islam*

IN THE SIXTH century, when Judaism had been driven out of Palestine and Christianity was torn between the Churches of Rome and Constantinople, a third religion arose in Western Asia. In the Arabian city of Mecca a trader named Mohammed declared himself to be the chosen Prophet of Allah, the One Almighty God, and implored his people to give up their pagan gods and follow him.

❙   Mecca was a meeting place for men of many nations, for it lay in Arabia, not far from the Red Sea, at the junction of the age-old caravan routes that skirted the desert and linked the Mediterranean countries of Egypt, Palestine, and Syria with Persia, India, and the Far East. It was famous for its markets, and was also a center of pilgrimage where the Bedouin desert dwellers gathered to worship pagan gods of the sky and earth. They sacrificed animals at a sacred Black Stone, enshrined in an ancient cube-shaped building called the Kaaba, drew water from a Holy Well, and bartered their wares in the nearby bazaars.

The Arabian desert was thinly populated by wandering tribesmen who spoke roughly the same language, but were otherwise fiercely independent. They did not try to cultivate the parched land, but bred camels and goats for a living. They also demanded dues from traveling merchants in return for a safe passage, or raided unwary caravans and seized the goods. From time to time the Bedouin fought as mercenaries in the armies of neighboring nations, and because they were brave and accustomed to desert warfare they were greatly in demand by foreign rulers. Before the coming of Mohammed there had never been any kind of unity between the tribes. Mecca, the birthplace of Mohammed, was one of the few places where, in the month of pilgrimage, a truce was proclaimed, tribal feuds were set aside, and for a brief space people were free to worship their gods in peace.

Mohammed was born in A.D. 570, a member of a humble branch of the Koreish tribe which ruled Mecca and the surrounding countryside. His childhood was clouded with sadness and poverty. His father died before his birth and his mother when he was six years old. He was brought up among wandering shepherds by his grandfather, a tough old warrior who lived and died a pagan, and his uncle who was later converted to Mohammed's religion.

When Mohammed grew up he joined a trading caravan and after a few years went to work for a rich widow named Khadija. He traveled with her camel trains from Mecca to the Mediterranean, and it is possible that he talked to Jews and Christians along the way and learned to respect their belief in a single God. In those days traders had to drive a good bargain and also to defend their goods against armed raiders. It seems that Mohammed proved himself both honest and courageous. He was a rather serious and lonely young man, tactful with his superiors and conscientious in his work. At the age of twenty-five he married the widow, Khadija. Though she was fifteen years older it was a very happy marriage, only marred by the death of their two baby sons. Polygamy was an accepted Arab custom, but while Khadija lived Mohammed never took another wife. After she died, he married eight times in a desperate, but unsuccessful, effort to produce a son and heir to carry on his work.

When he was nearly forty years old Mohammed began to have dreams and visions. He went off alone into the desert to meditate, and during these days of solitude he fell into trances and received heavenly revelations. He returned home convinced that he had been chosen as a messenger of God, to proclaim his ways and pronounce his will. The people of Mecca jeered at Mohammed's new faith, but Khadija believed in her husband and cared for him tenderly when he was shaken by emotion and ecstasy. Mohammed delivered his message in plain words: "There is no god but Allah. All others are false and their idols must be destroyed." Never then, or at any other time, did he claim divinity for himself or the power to perform miracles. He acted simply as a humble prophet, carrying a warning of divine judgment from a sovereign God to a people who were tormented by strife and bloodshed.

Most of the Koreish tribe refused to accept Mohammed's words of warning and were openly hostile. But the Prophet was undaunted. He preached twice a day to his family and a few lowly followers and led them in prayer. Gradually he collected a little band of firm believers who were known as Moslems.

In 622, he took his faithful flock to the city of Medina, two hundred miles north of Mecca, to escape the persecution and ridicule of his own tribe. This migration was a momentous event. It is known as the Hjira, or departure, and it marks the beginning of the Islamic era. In the same way that the Christian calendar dates from the birth of Christ, the Moslem calendar begins with the Hjira.

In Medina he laid the foundations of the Islamic religion. Islam is an Arab word meaning "submission to the will of God." There are five Pillars, or Foundations, of Islam and the first is faith. The other four are prayer, almsgiving, fasting, and pilgrimage.

When Mohammed built the first mosque, from a slender tower, or minaret, high on the roof the *muezzin,* or crier, sum-

The muezzin calls

moned the faithful to prayer. Five times a day—at sunset, by night, at dawn, noon, and in the afternoon—his voice rang out: "God is most great, I testify that there is no God but Allah. I testify that Mohammed is God's Apostle. Come to prayer. Come to security. God is most great." At dawn he added that prayer is more important than sleep.

Mosques are dedicated to prayer, for the word mosque means "prostration," and in every period of worship there is a time when Moslems touch the ground with their foreheads in deep obeisance. Most mosques are built around a courtyard and the minarets rise from a gallery at the base of the dome. The holy sanctuary is a rounded recess, and those who face it know that they are looking toward the Holy City of Mecca. There are no statues and no altar, and the only decorations on the walls are sacred sayings written in Arabic script. When the *muezzin* calls, devout Moslems cover their heads and enter the mosque barefoot. If they are too far away they simply turn toward Mecca, spread the prayer rugs which they always carry, and worship where they happen to be, regardless of the outside world.

Almsgiving is the third Pillar of Faith. Every good Moslem is obliged to contribute to the upkeep of the mosques and help the unfortunate and needy. Charity is a stepping stone on the road to Paradise. In Moslem countries there is no shame in begging, for it provides the rich with an opportunity, which they would not have otherwise, to show generosity and human kindness to the poor.

The rules of fasting, the fourth Pillar of Faith, are strict

Moslems at prayer

and hard to follow, even for devout Moslems. They may not at any time drink alcohol, or eat certain foods such as pork. In the month of Ramadan, the fifth of the Moslem calendar, the rules of fasting are more exacting than at any other time. This month is especially holy because tradition holds that it was then that the Koran, the holy book of Islam, was sent down by God as guidance for the people. During Ramadan, Moslems are not allowed to eat, drink, or smoke from the first gleam of sunrise until darkness falls. In the hot countries where most of them live, it is a stern test of obedience and self-control not to take a single sip of water during the whole day.

The fifth Pillar of Faith is pilgrimage. Mohammed told the people that Allah decreed that they should all visit the Holy City of Mecca at least once before they died. The twelfth month of every year is the appointed time for pilgrimage, and more than a million people make the sacred journey. Some come from neighboring countries, but others travel thousands of miles to seek forgiveness for their sins and gain a place among the elect of Allah. They used all to travel on foot or by camel, moving slowly across the desert tracks with mounting excitement as they neared the hallowed ground. Now many arrive in pilgrim ships, airplanes, or lorries, but their piety is no less and, with the high cost of transport, their sacrifice is often very great indeed.

Mohammed called his followers "Companions" and addressed them as "the Faithful." Those who did not embrace Islam he stamped as infidels and did everything he could to convert them either by persuasion or by force. He urged the Faithful to surrender themselves utterly to God, and to accept with fortitude the trials and tribulations of life, trusting always in his love and mercy. The Prophet preached that because God was all-powerful he was also ever-present. Mohammed dismissed all fear of dying, for death opens the gateway to Paradise, a land of green meadows, shady trees, and cooling streams, where all those who obey God's will shall surely enter. On the other hand the Prophet warned evildoers that Hell awaited them, a yawning cavern filled with scorching fires and stifling black smoke.

Islam has no ordained priesthood and men are not expected to dedicate their lives to any Church, for Church and State are merged in a single body. As the Law of Islam covers the whole of life, every duty is an act of dedication to God. Therefore men marry and have families, and the leaders of the faith are simply learned scholars versed in religious matters. Moslems do not profess their faith in the form of a creed, neither do they celebrate any sacraments such as the Christian Holy Communion. Before the coming of Mohammed the Arabs had no sacred literature. They worshiped their pagan gods according to unwritten customs and had no graven laws like the Hebrews, or Collections of Knowledge like the Hindus, or myths of Olympic gods like the Greeks.

The sacred book of Islam is the Koran, the word of Allah spoken to his Prophet. It is not known how much of the Koran was collected in writing during Mohammed's life. Undoubtedly some sections were inscribed on palm leaves, stones, and the bones of animals. The remainder was recited by professional memorizers who played an important part in Arab life. They were the historians, actors, storytellers, and journalists of that day. They traveled constantly and wherever they spoke, they were listened to with rapt attention.

When Mohammed died, war was widespread in Arab countries, and his followers were terrified that the words of Allah would be lost forever. They resolved to make a lasting record, and it is said that Zeid, a slave whom the Prophet had freed and adopted as his own son, undertook the treasured task.

The Koran is written in Arabic, in a form of rhythmic prose, impossible to translate without destroying its beauty. It has much in common with the Torah and the Bible, for Islam does not deny Old Testament teaching. The Arabs, like the Jews, trace their descent from Abraham—not through Isaac, but through Ishmael, another son. The lives of Isaac and Jacob, Joseph and Moses, Solomon and David, are faithfully portrayed in the Koran. Jesus Christ is treated with respect as a child of Mary, a messiah and a prophet, but not as the mystical Son of God.

The Koran is about the same length as the Christian New Testament. It used to be the duty of every Arab child to learn it by heart from beginning to end but recently teachers realized that this task imposed such a strain on their pupils that there was no time left for any other kind of education, and they lightened the burden. But each Moslem can repeat long passages of the Koran and does so on every public and private occasion. In every Moslem country but Turkey, the

Koran is still printed in Arabic. The volumes are so holy that no other book or any object must ever rest on them.

In Mohammed's day, and for centuries afterward, Moslem women have not had the same rights as the men. Heavily veiled, like Hindu women, they have been kept in *purdah* and prevented from taking part in public affairs. Their social life has been separate from that of Moslem men. Until recently a girl's only ambition in life was to find a kind husband and present him with handsome sons. Most parents did not think it necessary to give their daughters an education, even if they could afford it, for a woman's place was in the home. Nevertheless, throughout the age of Islam there have been a sprinkling of women who were well able to read and write, and some women have been recognized as saints. Today the scene is changing and Moslem women are emerging from their enforced seclusion. Western ideas are filtering through the Moslem world. The harem where rich Moslems kept their wives does not fit in with modern life, or a veil with Western dress.

A few years after the Hjira, the pattern of Islam was set and Mohammed made many converts in Medina. From this time onward he displayed the determination, the talent for statesmanship, and the personal magnetism that made him famous. He recruited men to his cause who were both loyal and obedient and took his place among them as an uncrowned king. But this he felt was only the beginning, and he never lost sight of his dream of all Arabs living peacefully together within a single faith. In the end Islam extended far beyond Arabia, carried by force in what he termed a "Holy War."

There were in the city of Medina a number of Jews who had fled from Roman persecution in Jerusalem. They had arrived penniless, but through sound agricultural knowledge and sustained hard work they had become landowners and merchants. At first these Jewish exiles welcomed Mohammed and recognized their own teaching in his words. However, when they discovered that he claimed a personal revelation from Allah, had laid down new laws, and paid homage to Mecca instead of Jerusalem, they turned against him. When they refused to fight in his army Mohammed drove them from the city and confiscated their goods. He was planning to make an assault on Mecca and he was very short of money and men. One Jewish tribe, suspected of treachery, he put to death in cold blood, a crime which has long been held against him.

In a series of raids, skirmishes, and battles against the Koreish tribe, Mohammed's meager forces suffered heavy loss, but escaped final defeat. He gained a reputation for valor and skill in war which greatly strengthened Moslem faith and won him new converts.

In 629, during the month of pilgrimage when a truce was declared between the warring tribes, Mohammed visited Mecca. A year later he brought an army and entered the city without serious opposition. He led his followers seven times around the Kaaba, touching the Black Stone with his staff, and calling on the Meccans to discard their pagan gods and bow down to Allah. He cast out hundreds of idols and it is said that he left only two pictures on the walls, those of Christ and the Virgin Mary, evidently painted by early Christian artists.

Mohammed knew his own people, and in his hour of triumph he did not try to change their ways too suddenly. He sanctified the Kaaba, and dedicated the ancient pagan shrine to Allah. He proclaimed that Mecca was the most Holy City of Islam and swore that from that day onward no infidel should enter its gates, a law which is still rigidly observed. The Korcish people were greatly impressed by Mohammed's success. They were warriors by nature and willingly put their trust in a God who, in their eyes, stood for victory.

Mohammed died at the age of sixty-one, two years after the conquest of Mecca. His achievements were remarkable. He left no living heir, but a heritage of steadfast faith. From a small sun-baked city he founded a religion which spread around the world.

After Mohammed's death a series of successors, or caliphs, ruled the Islamic Empire; and Arab armies, fighting for the Faith, went from victory to victory. In a hundred years the voice of the *muezzin,* calling Moslems to prayer, rang out from Spain to India. Though Moslem commanders were inspired by religious fervor, they owed many of their victories to the weakness of the surrounding nations and the harsh rule of Christian sovereigns. In many cities the Arabs were hailed as liberators, and in the Byzantine strongholds of Damascus and Jerusalem, resistance soon crumbled and the garrisons surrendered. In Jerusalem a Moslem caliph built a fine mosque on the site of Solomon's temple and named it the Dome of the Rock. It is especially sacred because of a legend that on this spot Mohammed tethered his winged horse, El Burak, the night before he mounted him and rode swiftly away to Paradise.

In 718, the Arabs launched a formidable attack against the Byzantine capital of Constantinople. They were decisively repulsed by a young Christian emperor, and Constantinople remained a bastion of Christianity in the midst of Islamic power until it was finally overwhelmed by Ottoman Turks in the fifteenth century.

Arab armies overran Egypt and captured Alexandria with its valuable library and famous university. They occupied Cairo and gazed with wonder at the mighty pyramids, for Arabia had nothing to compare with them. In general the conquered people did not find Moslem rule too oppressive. The caliphs did not have enough men trained in government to administer every city and the Islamic code of laws was less rigid and far-reaching than the Roman. They sent out officers to levy tribute and recruit men for fresh campaigns, and built mosques to the glory of Allah. Arab soldiers lived off the land; they looted tribal villages and took away the women and the camels. But gradually they married and settled down there, and adapted themselves to foreign customs. Everywhere the Moslems went, they spread their faith and the Arabic language which is still spoken in these regions today.

While the Arab Empire was in the making, the religious policy of the caliphs was clear. Pagans were given no choice between conversion to Islam and death. But if Jews and Christians were prepared to pay the tax of unbelievers they could

Mosque of the Sultan Hassan in Cairo

worship as they wished. Moslems called them "The People of the Book" and respected their beliefs. It was hard for most tribesmen to raise the money to buy religious freedom, and Islam was a simple faith which they could understand. So, in the course of time, many Byzantine Christians turned to Islam, though most Jews clung stubbornly to their ancient scriptures. In Egypt the Copts, a people descended from the original inhabitants of the Nile lands, formed a Christian minority and have kept the Coptic Church in Egypt, and also in Ethiopia, separate from the surrounding religions to this day.

The caliphs made their capital first in Damascus and later, when they had subdued the country which is now Iraq, they moved it to Baghdad. Moslem chiefs from North Africa, who ruled over people known as the Moors, crossed the Mediterranean and landed in Spain with little opposition. A Moorish general set up a rival capital in the city of Cordova, the most western outpost of Islam, declared himself a caliph, and reigned with dazzling pomp and pageantry. In the eighth century Cordova was the finest city in Europe, far richer than Rome. Foreign ambassadors marveled at the mosques, libraries, and public baths built of gleaming marble at a time when London and Paris were clusters of rough stone buildings.

The Moslem advance in Europe was finally arrested at Poitiers in western France. On a cold winter's day in 732, Charles Martel, king of the Franks and grandfather of the Emperor Charlemagne, defeated a Moorish army, ill-equipped for fighting so far from the desert. Moslem forces never ventured north again.

When the armies of Islam turned east, they were confronted by the Persian Empire, the greatest power in Western Asia, with its ancient capital at Babylon. Persia had been fighting a losing battle against Roman expansion and had already lost Palestine and many other early conquests. The Persian armies were no match for the fiery might of Islam. In 641, nine years after the death of Mohammed, the Persian Empire collapsed.

The Moslems not only crushed the Persian state but also the religion. Since prehistoric times the people had followed the teaching of Zoroaster who, it is thought, lived about the same time as Buddha. He founded a religion based on the universal battle between good and evil, the pursuit of truth and purity, and faithful service to one God. Persian priests, known as the Magi, collected Zoroaster's sayings in a sacred book, the Avesta. They linked his moral teaching with ancient customs, built fire-temples in his name, and conducted services before altars where a sacred flame burned constantly. A few Zoroastrians managed to escape Moslem persecution and crossed the mountains to India. There they settled, and for twelve hundred years these Persians, or Parsees as they are called in India, have taken a leading part in public life and won respect for their culture and good works.

When they had subdued Persia, Moslem rulers pressed on into northern India, first in a series of sharp raids and finally in massed invasions. They converted some Hindus to Islam by the sword and the spear, but they were not strong enough to extend Moslem rule to the southern states of India. For hun-

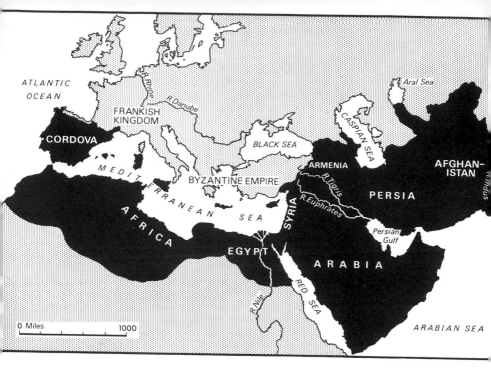

The spread of Islam circa A.D. 800

dreds of years, until Britain took over much of the country early in the eighteenth century, Moslem sultans and Hindu princes were continually battling for supremacy.

While Moslem armies fought on the fringes of the vast Arab Empire, Baghdad blossomed into a capital of beauty and learning. Wealth flowed in from subject states and the caliphs used it for the glory of Islam. They built splendid palaces, magnificent mosques, and an excellent university. Baghdad was a glorious city, its buildings richly decorated with glowing colors and a forest of slender minarets rising to the sky.

Ambitious men came from all over Western Asia to study

under the spreading cloak of Islam. Poets and painters, philosophers and scientists, craftsmen and merchants, architects and builders, astronomers, mathematicians, and geographers came to Baghdad, bringing their skill and knowledge. They wrote exquisite poetry, studied the thoughts and the actions of men, charted the heavens and the earth, produced lovely paintings, pottery, and gleaming rugs, dug canals, erected viaducts, and invented the numerals which many countries use today. But perhaps most important of all, Arab scholars translated Greek literature and thought into Arabic, and bookbinders set the precious manuscripts in covers of fine leather stamped with gold to preserve them for posterity.

The Arab Empire lasted from 700 to 1100, and during this time Europe was overwhelmed by barbarian invasions and plunged into a dark age of ignorance and fear. For four hundred years Arab civilization kept the torch of learning alight and guarded a store of knowledge which would otherwise have been lost forever.

Islam is the youngest of the great living religions and it has increased steadily in numbers and influence until there are over four hundred million Moslems in the world today. It is, like Buddhism and Christianity, a missionary faith winning fresh converts every year, particularly in Africa. About a hundred and forty million Africans live in the region south of the Sahara Desert, and until the nineteenth century they worshiped gods of nature and the spirits of their ancestors. In the last hundred years approximately one third have adopted Islam and one third Christianity.

A modern mosque in Tunisia

Islam has remained truer to its original form than any other world religion. This is probably due to the fact that it was from the beginning a direct and simple faith, for Mohammed did not demand more of his followers than he thought they could attain; and also because most Moslems have continued to live in hot and comparatively poor countries, in a climate and conditions not far removed from those in which the Prophet worked and taught. The voice of the *muezzin* calling the people to prayer and the fellowship of the Mecca pilgrimage have contributed to Islamic unity.

Now Moslems are face to face with a rapidly changing world. The discovery of oil in Middle Eastern lands has brought sudden wealth to isolated desert regions. Arab *sheikhs* who formerly owned a few flocks of sheep or goats, or a string of camels, became multi-millionaires overnight. Industry and education are spreading to the most remote corners of the Moslem world. Moslem statesmen are in the forefront of world affairs, merchants prominent in international trade, and women demanding equality and freedom.

Many Islamic leaders are aware of this challenge. They have adapted certain customs, such as the veiling of women and polygamy, for these were not essential to Islamic belief. Moslems are a powerful force in many nations today, with a proud heritage of culture. To most Moslems their faith is a tower of strength and those who are farsighted are seeking ways of retaining their basic beliefs and yet advancing with the march of time.

11 · *From Constantine to Communism*

SITUATED AT THE crossroads of Europe and Asia, the Byzantine Empire led a stormy and perilous existence. Brief intervals of peace and prosperity were followed by long periods of war. For eleven hundred years Constantinople stood like a faithful sentinel, defending Christendom in turn against the attacks of barbarian, Persian, and Moslem foes. The city was a natural fortress, standing high on a promontory protected on three sides by the Sea of Marmora, the Bosporus Straits, and the Black Sea. Successive emperors built an imposing line of battlements to block a land attack, and they proved almost impregnable.

In the year 518, Justinian the Great ascended the Byzantine throne. He was an able diplomat, a skilled lawyer, and a gallant warrior. He inherited all Constantine's dreams of a mighty Christian realm, and fought for thirty years to extend his dominions. But he is best remembered today for the legal code which he introduced throughout the Empire and the magnificent churches which he caused to be built. The most majestic of all was the cathedral of Hagia Sophia, meaning "Holy Wisdom," in Constantinople, a supreme example of Byzantine and Western art combined. Ten thousand workmen were employed on the construction and in six years they completed the shrine, the crowning glory of Justinian's reign. Rare marbles and gleaming glass reflected the sunlight from without and the flames of hundreds of candles from within. Vivid mosaics carpeted the floor and sparkled in the vaulted ceiling. The altar and pulpit were faced with gold, silver, and ivory, and inset with precious stones. The Patriarch of Constantinople sat on a throne of solid silver and served the bread and wine in the sacrament of Holy Communion from vessels of beaten gold. The vestments of the clergy and the hangings of the cathedral were of finest silk and velvet, richly embroidered. Painted panels, or icons, of Christ, the Virgin Mary, and holy saints hung before the altar, glistening with jewels. The air was heavy with incense, and visitors from many lands were spellbound by the beauty of the "great church" of Hagia Sophia.

Justinian died in 565, five years before the birth of Mohammed. In the following centuries, Christians and Moslems fought for supremacy in Western Asia until in 1070 a new enemy appeared on the horizon, and fierce tribes of Seljuk Turks stormed in from the Far East, bent on conquest. They broke down Arab resistance, seized Syria and Palestine, and defeated the Byzantine forces with fearful slaughter in the country that is now Armenia. The Greek and Latin Churches had officially broken off relations some years before, but it was clear to Alexius, the ruling Byzantine emperor, that Constantinople was the next target. So he swallowed his pride and sent an urgent message to the head of the Western Church,

Pope Urban II in Rome, asking for Christian help against a pitiless and powerful enemy.

Urban responded instantly to the appeal. He was an ardent priest and a clever politician. He saw in the weakness of the Byzantine Empire a chance of making Rome once more the most powerful city in Christendom. He organized a campaign to raise a force of crusaders to fight a Holy War to recapture Jerusalem and other Christian cities from the hands of unbelievers. Urban toured northern Italy and southern France making impassioned speeches, calling on knights and commoners to take up arms for the Church. Everywhere the Pope went, crowds gathered to listen to him and, deeply stirred by his eloquence, enlisted under the Christian banner. He enrolled a host of crusaders and, after every gathering, distributed crosses for soldiers to wear on brow and breast.

In fact, until this time many Moslem caliphs had acted with tolerance and restraint, and had permitted Christian pilgrims to visit their holy places without interference. When a fanatical Moslem ruler destroyed the Church of the Holy Sepulcher, which stood in Jerusalem on the spot where the crucified body of Christ had rested, other Moslems paid to have it rebuilt. But with the onslaught of the Seljuk Turks, the situation had changed. They were far less civilized than the Arabs and their hold on Jerusalem was a real threat to Christian worshipers.

In 1096, the First Crusade set out under the command of a French nobleman, Godfrey de Bouillon, an able soldier and a faithful Christian. The ranks were filled almost entirely with Frenchmen, drawn from many walks of life. Some were devout Christians prepared to lay down their lives for the sacred cause, others were freed serfs released from bondage for the Crusade, and others were professional soldiers, adventurers, and fortune hunters. There was little discipline or organization, and many crusaders took their wives along with them for company. They began the march south poorly supplied for such an arduous undertaking. They soon ran out of funds and food, and began to pillage the countryside. Townspeople learned to close their gates and man their defenses as the crusaders approached. By the time the defenders of the Christian faith reached Constantinople, many had fallen by the wayside and others were destitute and ill. However, in 1097, about thirty thousand men crossed the Bosporus Straits and pressed on toward Jerusalem. They wore leather jackets and heavy chain armor. No one had prepared them for waterless wastes and desert heat, and they suffered agonies from thirst and exhaustion.

It was fortunate for the crusaders that the strength of the Seljuk Turks was already spent and that the Moslem armies were also exhausted by previous battles and short of good generals. The Christian forces succeeded in capturing the Syrian city of Antioch and, two years after they left Constantinople, the remnants of the First Crusade stood before the walls of Jerusalem. They laid siege to the city for a hundred days until the hungry garrison surrendered. Then Godfrey de Bouillon led his tired but triumphant men through the gates. This conquest of Christian arms ended in a savage massacre. Thousands of Moslems and the few Jews who remained in the city were relentlessly slaughtered. When the killing died down, Godfrey de Bouillon was elected Defender of the Holy Sepulcher to rule over a sovereign state of Jerusalem.

The Christian occupation of Jerusalem lasted until 1187 when Saladin, a famous Moslem warrior, led his army against Palestine. A Second Crusade, hurriedly assembled, failed to stem his advance and he captured Jerusalem. Saladin showed far more good sense and mercy than his Christian enemies. He demanded pieces of gold as a sign of surrender but spared the lives of his conquered foes. He removed the Christian Cross from the Dome of the Rock, put the Crescent which had become a symbol of Islam in its stead, and reconsecrated the mosque to Islam. At the same time he granted Christians free entry into Jerusalem, provided they left their arms outside the city gates.

A Third Crusade under the English king, Richard Coeur de Lion, set out for Jerusalem, but Saladin's defenses held fast. When he died European ambitions revived. In 1202, an expedition set out from Venice with the Cross as its emblem and greed at its heart. By this time enterprising European merchants had realized what the Orient had to offer. The crusaders had revealed sources of wealth hitherto undreamed of. They had robbed not only Moslem mosques but also Christian churches, and returned home loaded with treasure. With mounting excitement European traders priced the gold and silver, carpets and tapestries, silks and velvets, scents and spices, diamonds, pearls, and rubies which the crusaders laid before them.

The Fourth Crusade aimed not at the deliverance of Jerusalem from Moslem rule, but at the subjection of the Christian city of Constantinople. The Pope had no means of preventing this outrage. The defenders of Constantinople were weakened by internal rivalry for the imperial throne and the crusaders captured the city with little bloodshed. Then the looting began. Soldiers thronged the streets rifling churches, palaces, and bazaars. They even tore apart the high altar of Hagia Sophia and carried off the sacred relics. They sacked libraries and museums, destroying priceless manuscripts in a mad search for hidden spoils. This was the final major Crusade and it left a lasting stain on Christian consciences. In 1291 Antioch, the last remaining Christian conquest, was recaptured by a Moslem army.

The crusaders had failed in their noble purposes. Jerusalem remained in Moslem hands and hundreds of Christian churches and Moslem mosques lay in ruins. The high ideals and brave endeavor of Christian knights withered away, and two hundred years of Holy War left a heritage of deep distrust between followers of the different religions, matched only by the bitterness which divided the Churches of Rome and Constantinople. It was a high price to pay for the discovery of Oriental riches which in the course of time brought learning, prosperity, and loveliness to many European homes.

In the fifteenth century a new tide of invasion broke over Western Asia. Hordes of fighting Ottoman Turks advanced from the borders of China to the shores of the Black Sea, and both Christian and Arab armies collapsed before them. The last of the Byzantine emperors died in defense of Constantinople and the Turks captured the city and installed a sultan in his stead. They speedily occupied Syria, Egypt, Palestine, and all Arabia, for the might of the Arab Empire had faded away. The Turkish conquerors adopted the Moslem faith and ruled the Arab world in comparative peace for the next four hundred years.

Constantinople became a Moslem city and the Byzantine Empire ceased to exist. But the Greek Orthodox Church, the Eastern section of Christianity, survived, for by this time it had won many converts and gained a firm foothold in Eastern Europe.

To the north of Byzantium the vast territory now known as the Soviet Union remained for many centuries an untamed wilderness. Dark forests and sweeping plains, or steppes, stretched from the Baltic to the Black Sea. The only highways were the rivers and the only inhabitants scattered Slavs, forest people who lived in clearings by the river banks and bartered honey and hides with passing traders.

In the ninth century Norse seamen set out from Scandinavia on a series of raids which carried them deep into Russia. These Viking warriors came to plunder but stayed to rule. They brought with them their own laws and religion, and at the end of the tenth century a Viking named Vladimir reigned as Grand Duke of Kiev, in southern Russia. True to the tradition of his people Vladimir was a pagan. He worshiped Odin, and Thor, a god of thunder and lightning, and Perun, a fearsome god of war. After a victory Vladimir sacrificed enemy captives at the feet of a great wooden image of Perun.

Though Vladimir collected tribute from the people of Kiev and the surrounding countryside, he found his subjects unruly and rebellious. Like many other sovereigns he looked with admiration and envy at the city of Constantinople, still in his day the capital of an organized empire and the center of an established faith. The Grand Duke of Kiev resolved to introduce law and order in his own domains with the help of an established church. Having reached this important decision, he then set out to find the religion best suited to his purpose and most acceptable to his people.

Kiev lies at the junction of the rivers Dnieper and Desna, where merchants gathered to sell their wares and priests came to spread their beliefs. An ancient legend relates how Vladimir examined them all in turn before he made his choice. He was impressed by the conquests of the Moslem armies, but the laws of Islam forbade strong drink so he refused to obey them. He respected the learning of Judaism and the efficiency of Hebrew merchants, but when he heard that the Jews were wanderers on the face of the earth, with no country they could call their own, this seemed an unforgivable sign of weakness. He was attracted by the culture and discipline of the Church of Rome, but when missionaries told him that submission to the will of God and obedience to the Pope were far more important than allegiance to an earthly ruler, Vladimir was not prepared to surrender his princely authority. He was familiar with the teaching of the Eastern patriarchs, but he sent trusted envoys to Constantinople to study the working relationship between Church and Empire. Vladimir's messengers returned filled with admiration for everything they had seen. They reported that the Byzantine emperor appointed a priest to care for the spiritual welfare of his people, but continued to hold the reins of government.

They related too that when they entered the portals of Hagia Sophia, the interior was so glorious that "they did not know whether they were in Heaven or on earth." Vladimir hesitated no longer. In the Greek Orthodox Church he had found a faith which excited his senses and fulfilled his needs. In 988, he adopted Christianity, married the sister of the ruling Byzantine emperor, dismissed all his other wives, commanded his people to be baptized in the River Dnieper, and built Christian churches in Kiev.

Early in the thirteenth century catastrophe struck the dukedom of Kiev. Hordes of Mongol horsemen, under the leadership of a great chief, Genghis Khan, stormed in from the east and laid waste every town and city in southern Russia. For two hundred years princes and dukes throughout Russia were forced to pay homage and tribute to Mongol khans, or kings, at Sarai on the banks of the Volga River, where they had established a capital decked with barbaric splendor. When internal strife weakened Mongol power in the fifteenth century, Moscow became the center of Russian government and religion. With the blessing of high dignitaries of the Church, Russian rulers took the titles first of Grand Duke and later Czar of Moscow and All Russia. Church and state were closely linked, sharing the growing importance of a united country. The Church changed its name and character from the Greek to the Russian Orthodox Church, the bishops were chosen from among Russian instead of Greek priests, and the services were conducted in the Russian language. Patriarchs of the Greek Orthodox Church had claimed that Constantinople was "the new Rome." After

Christmas service in Russia

the fall of the Byzantine Empire, the Russian patriarchs christened Moscow "the third Rome," capital of Holy Russia. By this time the Russian Orthodox Church had become the strongest Church of Eastern Christianity, independent of Constantinople and far removed from the Church of Rome.

From the days of Vladimir the people of Russia have been deeply religious. Until the Bolshevik Revolution in 1917, most of the population worked on the land and village life centered around the Church. Men and women labored as serfs on the estates of wealthy landlords and spent most of their lives on the verge of starvation. But they were uplifted from the grim realities of the day to day struggle for existence by the love of Christ, the hope of salvation, and the extreme beauty of the Church ritual. The Russian Orthodox services brought comfort and brightness to millions of simple, trusting peasants. They found in the Church help for a present and hope for a future life.

Before the twentieth century there were few schools in Russia, and three-quarters of the population could not read or write. They turned to the clergy whenever they were troubled or in doubt and listened to their words with unquestioning faith. In every humble cottage an oil lamp burned before an icon of the Blessed Virgin or the patron saint of the region. Men and women coming in from the fields paused to bow or curtsy at the little shrine that sanctified their home.

Religious festivals in Russia were colorful occasions. People looked forward with eager expectation to Christmas and Easter. In all the villages little churches with onion-shaped spires were decked with branches of fir and thronged with worshipers. Even the poorest families managed somehow to make a candle of beeswax to burn on the altar. Perhaps the greatest church events of all were the weddings. They took place in the autumn, because people spent the long dark winters indoors around smoky peat fires trying to keep warm, and in the spring and summer they were too busy with the crops. The parents of the bride prepared the best feast they could possibly afford and invited the whole village to a celebration that sometimes lasted for three days and nights.

Because the working people of Russia were cut off from Europe by distance, language, and religion, they had little contact with the Church of Rome and no share in the material progress and the learning that began in Italy with the Renaissance, or revival of learning, in the fourteenth century and spread slowly through the other realms of Christendom.

It was only in the seventeenth century that the reigning czar, Peter the Great, turned to the West for progressive ideas to strengthen his backward empire. He fought his way to Western Europe, secured the Baltic ports, and introduced some modern inventions and ideas into Russia. He built the magnificent new capital of St. Petersburg, a name now changed to Leningrad, as a symbol of his success. But the long-suffering peasants paid the price of imperial ambitions in toil, taxes, and blood. Though Russia became a power in Europe, they were worse off than ever before.

In addition to the political changes Peter the Great reshaped the constitution of the Russian Orthodox Church. Before he came to the throne Church and State had worked together, and the Patriarch of Moscow had presided over a council that carried considerable weight in religious matters. When the Patriarch died in 1700, Peter postponed the election of a successor and the Russian Church became subject to the will of the czars, a state of affairs that lasted for more than two hundred years.

In the nineteenth century, revolutionary thought began to penetrate Russian minds. A small group of educated middle-class people openly denounced a regime where the court of the czar and the homes of the aristocrats were surrounded by excessive luxury while the peasants lived in hovels without a plot of ground they could call their own. The pent-up storm of discontent broke out under the pressure of the First World War. All through the winter of 1916–1917, news of heavy casualties on the Russo-German front brought despair to Russian homes. Every able-bodied man had been drafted and there were none left to cultivate the land. The wheat fields lay barren and the stocks of grain were exhausted. Bread lines grew longer and longer, and women stood in the windswept streets all night and then went home empty-handed. Spurred on by trained revolutionaries, the people arose in savage rebellion and murdered the czar with his entire family. In a wave of uncontrolled violence everyone of means or position in Russia lost their property and thousands their lives. The revolutionaries called themselves Bolsheviks, meaning "Men of the Majority." In November, 1917, under a leader who took the name of Lenin, they formed a government designed not only to rule Russia but also to convert the whole world to the political creed now known as Communism.

The Russian Church reacted immediately to the change of government, and representatives gathered in Moscow to elect a new Patriarch for the first time since the reign of Peter the Great. But revolutionary leaders took harsh action against the Church. They had seized power by force and they could not afford to recognize any other authority within the state. They regarded the Orthodox clergy as instruments of the hated czarist rule and determined to stamp out their influence. The Bolsheviks closed many churches and converted them into museums or places of entertainment, expelled the priests, and commandeered church property. They shut down monasteries and convents, and banned religious colleges or any Christian teaching in the schools.

During the next few years, by Communist decree, civil ceremonies replaced Christian marriages and Church festivals were abolished. A state calendar was drawn up with certain days set aside as national holidays for military parades and political rallies. People were compelled to work for ten-day stretches so that they could not observe Sunday as a regular day of prayer and rest. Children missed the presents that they had opened on the Eve of St. Nicholas, the patron saint of Russia, and in many parishes they were not even allowed to celebrate Christmas. A Union of the Godless staged mock processions, holding up the ancient ritual of the Orthodox Church to open ridicule. At the same time cunning propaganda treated would-be churchgoers with amused contempt as old-fashioned, simple-witted, and hopelessly unfit for life in that modern age. School children were directed to inform the authorities if their parents were practicing Christians. Belief in God was condemned as treason and punished accordingly. Under these conditions the Church lost almost all its rights, but though the Communist Party reigned supreme in every other sphere religious observance never entirely disappeared from Russia.

At the outbreak of the Second World War, the Russian Church was struggling for survival. When the Bolsheviks came to power there had been over fifty thousand churches functioning in Russia; in 1940 there were only a hundred, and every monastery and convent had been closed down. But despite the extreme persecution, at this time of desperate peril the remaining clergy instantly declared their patriotic loyalty to their country. As the German armies surged across the Russian frontier, Joseph Stalin, successor to Lenin and absolute dictator of the Soviet Union, softened the laws against the Christian religion, hoping to unite his own people and win sympathy and support for his war effort from other nations. A number of churches and a few religious training colleges were reopened. Gradually people overcame their fear and flocked to the services. Christian festivals were revived, and priests returned to their parishes and celebrated the Holy Eucharist with traditional ritual.

As news of these concessions filtered through the Iron Curtain, it was welcomed with relief and rejoicing by Christians in other lands. In 1945 the Russians enthroned with great pomp a new Patriarch of Moscow and invited high ranking clergy from friendly countries to attend the ceremony. During the next few years the Russian Orthodox Church was permitted to establish relations with neighboring Christian Churches, and in 1960 the Patriarch attended a pan-Orthodox conference in the Greek island of Rhodes. When the Soviet Union sent a delegation to the World Council of Churches in Delhi in 1961, it seemed that the dark days of the Russian Orthodox Church were ending.

Clergy of the Eastern Orthodox Churches meet at Rhodes

These high hopes have not been wholly fulfilled. A number of churches are open and filled to overflowing with congregations of young and old, but others have their doors locked and barred by government order, and in the 1960's fresh persecution endangered the future of the Russian Orthodox Church.

There are formidable barriers between Christian and Communist thinking. Membership in the Communist Party is a vital steppingstone to success in the Soviet Union today, and only atheists—people who declare that they do not believe in any God—are allowed to join it. Communism is at heart an anti-religious militant organization, dedicated to the service of the state. The Russian Orthodox Church is a deep and mystical faith dedicated to the service of God. But both in their different ways are working for the good of the Russian people. It may well be that in the course of time the Communist Party will soften its religious policy and that there will prove to be ample room for both creeds within the wide reaches of the Soviet Union.

12 · *The Christian Church of the West*

WHILE THE GREEK ORTHODOX CHURCH of Constantinople was struggling to establish Christianity in Asia, the Church of Rome was besieged by pagan peoples pouring into Europe from the north and east. These barbaric warriors occupied lands from the North Sea to the Nile. They were divided into tribes each with its own chieftain or king. The Angles, Jutes, and Saxons landed in Britain; while the Bavarians, Burgundians, Alemans, Franks, and other invaders took possession of central Europe. Fiercest of all, the Lombards and Gothic tribes stormed south through Italy and Spain.

Many pagans within the Roman Empire blamed these disastrous invasions on their fellow citizens who had abandoned Roman gods and adopted the Christian faith. Even a number of Christians were shaken by the crushing defeats. In 354, at this time of doubt and despair, St. Augustine, one of the greatest thinkers of the early Christian Church, was born at the Roman town of Hippo in North Africa. His father was pagan and his mother a devout Christian, but for many years he resisted her teaching.

Suddenly St. Augustine underwent an overwhelming mystical experience, and became an ardent Christian. He showed the people how the hand of God worked in everything and warned them that their defeats were due to sinfulness and sloth. He was gifted with remarkable vision and acquired a wide knowledge of the Hebrew scriptures and the Greek philosophers. He also recognized the importance of the newer Roman school of thought which was, by this time, replacing the Greek language and tradition of learning in Western Europe.

St. Augustine taught that the Church was the only divine authority in the world, and he set the pattern of a relationship between Church and State which lasted for hundreds of years. He uplifted the Christians of his own day by his absolute certainty of the power of heavenly grace, and his words have inspired Christian teachers ever since.

It was through the influence of men like this that, though Roman civilization declined, Christianity held its own against the barbarian onslaught. When Constantine founded the new imperial capital of Constantinople, many Christian clergy remained in Rome. Soon the Bishop of Rome began to call himself Pope, from the Latin word *Papa,* or Father, and in the fifth, century it became his official title. The Pope was accepted by Western Christians as their supreme leader, holder of the highest office in the Holy Bishopric of St. Peter, and the Vicar of Christ on earth. Many Roman citizens of wealth and ability who had formerly served the emperor now turned to the Pope instead. They were ordained as priests and contributed greatly to the growing prestige of the Christian Church.

In 481 Clovis, son of a Frankish nobleman, became king of

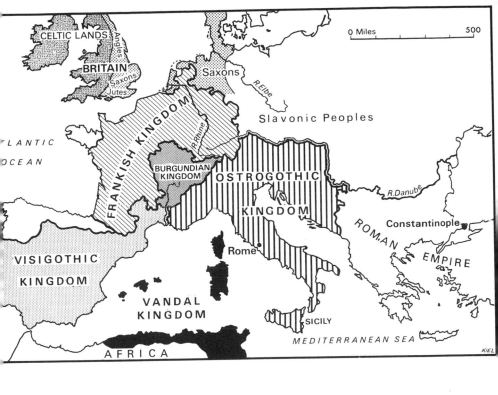

Barbarian kingdoms circa A.D. *500*

his tribe at the age of fifteen. He defeated rival chiefs and left the Rhineland to set up a new capital in Paris. There he founded the kingdom of France, which still bears the name of his people. In 496, Clovis adopted Christianity and the Church of Rome gained a powerful ally.

Three hundred years later Charlemagne, the most famous of all the Frankish monarchs, came to the throne and proved himself a great general and a fine statesman. He spent the forty-three years of his reign fighting to enlarge his kingdom and defend the Christian cause. His conquests were enormous. On Christmas Day in the year 800, Charlemagne attended the service at St. Peter's in Rome. The church was filled to overflowing with a stately gathering of kings, nobles, and clergy, who had traveled far to share the majesty and mystery of the Christmas celebration. As Charlemagne rose from his knees after receiving the Holy Eucharist, the Pope placed the imperial crown on his head. In a burst of jubilation the congregation hailed him: Charlemagne, great and peace-bringing emperor who rules the Holy Roman Empire. They rejoiced that dissention was ended, imperial glory restored, and that Christianity was moving from strength to strength.

The centuries that elapsed between the reign of Charlemagne and the year 1492, when Christopher Columbus discovered the New World, are known as the Middle Ages. During this time the barbarian invaders were gradually tamed. They changed their way of life and became law-abiding citizens, prudent landowners, able craftsmen, learned scholars, and ardent Christians.

The Church of Rome was largely responsible for this transformation. Bishops and priests went out into the wilds preaching of the love of God and charity among men. All over Europe they founded religious orders and built monasteries and convents, where by example and patient instruction they encouraged virtue and created a respect for learning.

Parish priests ministered to outlying communities but the monasteries were the main centers of religion. In addition they provided the colleges, hospitals, hotels, and libraries of their day. In candlelit cells and quiet cloisters holy men worked and

Eleventh-century pilgrim chapel at Le Puy in France

prayed, far from the turmoil of worldly strife. The abbots and monks were scholars, scribes, painters, astronomers, doctors, musicians, bankers, and farmers. In the convents nuns fasted and prayed, nursed the sick, fed the hungry, and gave the weary rest. Both monks and nuns were servants of God and counselors of men. People came to them for spiritual comfort and practical aid.

With infinite care and devotion to duty, members of the monastic orders copied down the writings of former scholars, and preserved them through a dark age of ignorance for the benefit of mankind. Medieval manuscripts, with their illuminated texts and exquisite drawings, display the skill and patience of these dedicated men, who also recorded local legends, historical events, medical prescriptions, and chants and prayers.

Many religious painters and sculptors depicted most vividly the prevailing Christian conception of life after death. According to the interpretation of that time of the Gospels and the Book of Revelation, the last book of the New Testament, every Christian would face a final judgment before the Son of God. If they obtained forgiveness of their sins they would enter the kingdom of Heaven and experience everlasting bliss. On the other hand a state of purgatory awaited those who had not yet atoned for their wrongdoing. Worst of all the unrepentant would be condemned to the horrors of Hell, where an evil presence known as Satan, or the devil, ruled over a realm of fire and torment. The minds of many medieval Christians were dominated by the fear of eternal damnation.

The earliest of the great monastic leaders was an Italian, St. Benedict of Nursia. He founded in the fifth century a Holy Order based on the highest Christian ideals and an intense desire to improve the lot of the people. On the towering height of Monte Cassino, south of Rome, he built a monastery where Benedictine monks in their black habits divided their time between fasting and prayer, studying the scriptures, and working in the surrounding fields. St. Benedict was pious but practical

The Crucifixion, from a fifteenth-century prayer book

and he showed remarkable moderation in his religious rules. He was followed by the Cistercians, the White Monks, whose regulations were far more severe, and later by the Trappists who, when they joined the order, took a vow of silence for the rest of their lives.

While St. Benedict labored in Italy St. Patrick, patron saint of Ireland, carried Christianity to the land of his boyhood. A hundred years later St. Columba crossed the Irish Sea and landed on the bleak isle of Iona, off the coast of Scotland, with twelve disciples. There with their own hands they hewed out the stone for a simple church and, determined to spread the gospel, set out on a series of hazardous missions to the mainland preaching to the pagan Picts and Scots.

Roman civilization in Britain was destroyed by barbarian invasion, and for a time paganism prevailed. At the end of the sixth century, Pope Gregory the Great faced the urgent task of reclaiming souls in Britain. He sent out St. Augustine, a Roman monk, on this distant mission to the wilds. Augustine landed on the Kentish coast in southern England with forty companions, and settled in Canterbury. By their virtuous life and earnest preaching these Christians made a profound impression on the heathen inhabitants, and by the end of the first year the king of Kent and ten thousand Saxons were baptized. Gradually, Christianity spread southward from Scotland and northward from Kent until the two streams met, and in 634 at the Synod of Whitby Britain became a Christian country, subject to the Church of Rome.

These dedicated missionaries set an example of religious zeal which was followed in many countries. In the eleventh century, St. Bruno, a German by birth, founded the Carthusian Order with its first monastery in a remote valley high in the French Alps.

In the thirteenth century, St. Francis of Assisi, renowned and beloved throughout the Christian world, created the Franciscan Order. He was the son of a rich Italian cloth merchant and had been brought up with other young gallants for an army career. When he heard the call of Christ, St. Francis renounced all his worldly possessions, and with a growing band of gray-clad preachers walked barefoot through the Italian countryside urging people to repent of their sins.

In the same century St. Dominic, a Spanish priest, founded the Dominican Order to train teachers and send them far afield on Christian missions. Outstanding among the Dominicans was St. Thomas Aquinas, a learned and pious man. His influence extended far beyond his own lifetime, and successive generations of priests and scholars have found in his writings a fund of humanity and knowledge which he gained from the teaching of Christ mingled with the reasoning of Aristotle, for he had a profound admiration for the Greek mind.

In order to carry out their work the Franciscan and Dominican Orders needed a new type of priest, who instead of withdrawing from the world to monastic retirement went out to work among the people and share their lives. These traveling preachers did not call themselves monks, a name derived from the Greek word meaning "alone," but took the title of brother, *fratello* in Italian and friar in English.

At the end of the twelfth century, an outstanding statesman and scholar was elected Pope. He took the name of Innocent III and raised the Papacy to the very zenith of its power. Innocent believed that the Church should dominate the State, and that the word of the Pope should override the dictates of emperors and kings. In 1215, he summoned over four hundred bishops, eight hundred abbots and priors, and kings, princes, and ambassadors from every country in Christendom to take part in the deliberations of the Roman Church. This Fourth Lateran Council was the greatest ecclesiastical assembly of the whole Middle Ages and its final pronouncements had a lasting effect on the future of Christianity.

One of the most important decrees gave the Popes the absolute right to appoint bishops to dioceses anywhere in Christendom, a power that was later ill-used by Popes less upright than Innocent himself. They sold Church livings to the highest bidder, regardless of the protests of the princes and parishioners concerned, and aroused indignation that, coupled with other grievances, led eventually to outright rebellion, the break-up of Western Christianity, and the formation of the Protestant Churches.

Other Lateran resolutions provided for the organized suppression of revolutionary groups within the Church, and severe penalties for men and women who voiced opinions out of keeping with official doctrine. These opinions were termed "heresy" and the people who expressed them "heretics."

Foremost among the sects which diverged from the Church were the Albigenses, so-called because they made their headquarters at the town of Albi in southern France. These heretics claimed that spiritual values were all that mattered, and rejected the Old Testament because it acknowledged the creation and existence of a material world. The Albigenses condemned everything worldly, branded sex as utterly evil and birth as a sinful misfortune. They abolished marriage, and if they had had their way the human race would have died out altogether. They decried the teaching of Christian clergy and defied Papal authority.

The leaders of Christendom undertook as a sacred duty the task of restoring heretics to the Christian fold. They hoped to accomplish it by peaceful means but, convinced of the righteousness of their cause, they did not exclude the use of force. So, in the thirteenth century, the Pope gave his consent to the setting-up of a high-powered system of reform and correction, known as the Inquisition. It was designed to cleanse the Church of Rome of the worldliness and indolence which had crept into the priesthood, and also to redeem Christians who had strayed from the true faith, save them from the horrors of purgatory and hell-fire, and lead them to salvation. When the Albigenses were silenced, courts of Inquisition were set up in other parts of France, Italy, and Germany to fortify faith in the Roman Catholic Church.

On the instructions of their superiors, friars of the Dominican and Franciscan Orders sought out heretics and brought them to trial. Some of the accused confessed quickly, hoping for pardon, while others were tortured until they acknowledged their guilt, but many died rather than recant. The sentences were pronounced publicly in the presence of clergy, magistrates, and local people who gathered to hear them. The judgment of the inquisitors was absolute and there was no court of appeal. Heretics were fined, imprisoned, strangled, or burned at the stake. Their lands were seized and their goods confiscated. Many inquisitors grew rich, and a share of the proceeds found its way into the Papal treasury.

Already in England a growing discontent at the extravagance and worldliness of the Church had been voiced by a forthright and courageous scholar, John Wycliffe. He trained a group of teachers to carry his message to the ordinary people and translated the Bible into English so they could understand it. Wycliffe was not opposed to the authority of the Pope and the clergy provided they were righteous, but he protested when they stepped into high office without personal merit. He also challenged the right of the Pope to levy tribute from every Christian community.

In the fourteenth century, the Italian people led the rest of Europe in a glorious revival of learning which has come down in history as the Renaissance. The seeds of knowledge stored by learned priests blossomed into a splendor of scholarship and art which spread through the Western world. Through the rediscovery of Greek writings, the wisdom and beauty of ancient Greece came to new life. As a result of the markets opened up by the Crusades, trade was booming and wealth widespread. Merchant princes became patrons of the Church and gave their patronage and financial support to architects who designed cathedrals of matchless beauty, and to artists and sculptors who decorated them with sacred paintings, murals, and statues.

At the same time, bishops built themselves luxurious palaces and lived more like princes than priests, and heads of Holy Orders acquired large estates. Simplicity had ceased to be a Christian ideal. But despite the prevailing grandeur, the prestige of the Popes had declined. Political quarrels had crept into the Papacy and for a time there had even been rival Popes, one in Rome and a second living in a palatial fortress in the French city of Avignon.

Also, for the first time, the Popes were short of money. The Renaissance had raised the standard of living and luxury was costly. When the Papacy was restored to Rome, the Popes found that they were not rich enough to keep up with the surrounding magnificence. They began to enlarge their incomes in ways which were far removed from early Christian aims and brought a bad name on the Church of Rome.

As the Renaissance spread through Europe, new ideas were born. In 1442, a German inventor had produced the first printing press. Other countries followed suit, and books on religion and history and the classics were published in many languages. With widening education people who were neither priests nor scholars were able to read them. They did not depend on the Church as the sole source of information and began to reason for themselves. It was not long before certain thoughtful Christians became aware that some high-ranking clergy were unworthy of the immense privilege and power they possessed.

The words of the English reformer John Wycliffe had rung out through Europe, and found eager support in the little country of Bohemia on the eastern frontier of Germany. At the capital of Prague John Huss, a young priest of peasant stock, taught at the university. He was a most virtuous man and a fine preacher. Huss criticized the laziness and ignorance of the Bohemian clergy and the shameful greed of the Roman Church. He tried to give his own people a Church based on the pure teaching of Christ and fiercely denied that he was a heretic. Huss was tried by the Inquisition and burned at the stake in 1415, but his spirit lived on.

In 1483 Martin Luther, the fiery leader of the German Reformation, was born in a simple home in the province of Saxony. He was ordained in the Augustine Order, founded according to the rule of St. Augustine of Hippo, and in the course of his duties made a pilgrimage to Rome, where he was scandalized by the low moral standards of the Holy City. Luther was a devout Christian and set out to cleanse the Church of Rome of corruption and hypocrisy. When he returned to Germany, he publicly condemned the means by which the Popes raised money for their own purposes. Above all he protested against the practice of auctioning Church livings and selling Indulgences, or pardons for sin. He was shocked to find that the Church now offered people a place in Heaven in return for a donation to the building of the grand new church of St. Peter in Rome. He preached passionately that only God could grant forgiveness, and that faith was the pathway to salvation. In place of the splendor and pomp of the Roman Church, Luther offered the German people simpler services in their own language which even the humblest member of the congregation could comprehend, and he translated the Bible into German. He loved music

The Church of St. Peter in Rome

and he introduced hymns so that they could all join in the singing. It was through Luther's protests against many Church practices that he and his followers were first called Protestants. He did not agree with the Church rule that priests should be forbidden to marry.

Luther concerned himself with the practical problems of the poor as well as their spiritual welfare. He protested against the heavy burden of Church taxes that the peasants had to bear and the fact that the clergy, however rich, paid no taxes at all. His words also appealed to princes and nobles who resented Papal interference in affairs of state, and looked with envious eyes at at the huge Church estates, and he won a large following.

While Luther thundered out his message in Germany, a learned writer named Erasmus from Holland and a peasant priest named Zwingli in Switzerland also led the minds and the spirits of Christian men and women toward reform.

In 1545, the Pope convened a council at the German city of Trent to introduce certain moral reforms and confirm the doctrines of the Roman Catholic Church. The proclamations of this Council have given guidance to Roman Catholic thought ever since.

In Italy and Spain the Reformation was strangled at birth by the Inquisition, but in France early in the sixteenth century John Calvin, one of the most intellectual Christians of his day, advocated a new form of religious society.

Calvin left France to escape the penalties for heresy and settled in Geneva. He was an austere character, intolerant of human weakness, upright, and intensely sincere. He worked with

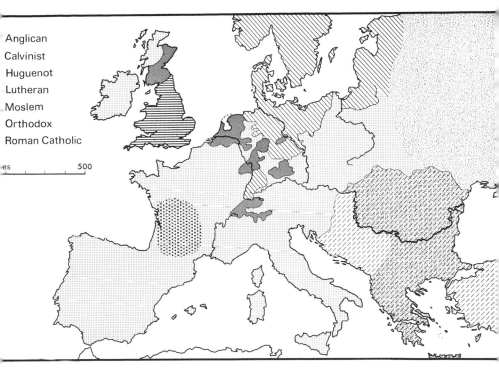

Anglican
Calvinist
Huguenot
Lutheran
Moslem
Orthodox
Roman Catholic

500

Christendom after the Reformation

unswerving resolve to purge the Church of outward display and restore what he believed was the simplicity of the first three centuries after Christ. Calvin wished to limit the membership of the Church to those who proved themselves worthy of it. In France, Calvin's followers called themselves Huguenots, and they were fiercely opposed by the forces of the Catholic Church. Towns, villages, and even families were divided in their beliefs and periodic religious wars swept through the country until in 1598 the Edict of Nantes gave the Huguenots freedom of worship.

Shortly afterward in Germany, Roman Catholic armies fought a war of counter-Reformation against the followers of Luther, and the people endured the prolonged agony and utter devastation of the Thirty Years' War. In 1648, at the Peace of Westphalia, it was finally agreed that the rulers of the many German principalities should be allowed to decide on a form of worship for their own subjects. When the princes made their choice, the German people were almost equally divided between the Reformed Churches and the Church of Rome.

The Reformation came to England with comparatively little bloodshed, and mainly for political reasons. In 1527, King Henry VIII applied to the Pope for permission to annul the marriage with his Spanish wife, Catherine of Aragon, as she had given him no son. The Pope refused to grant the royal request and Henry decided to free himself from Papal control. By an Act of Supremacy he proclaimed a Church of England, or Anglican Church, subject to the Crown. He executed two prominent supporters of the Church of Rome, Sir Thomas More and Cardinal Fisher, a community of Carthusian monks, and certain other Papal supporters who opposed his actions. But apart from isolated outbreaks of anger and rebellion, the English people accepted the new Church without undue excitement and were glad to be rid of foreign domination. They did not protest when the king dissolved the monasteries, seized their lands, and distributed to his supporters some of their wealth. Though Henry severed his connection with Rome, he did not share the religious fervor of the German and French reformers, or intend to introduce the Reformation into England. But once the Papal barriers were down, it was impossible to shut out the flood of religious controversy surging through Europe. Lutherans and Huguenots came to England and, after Henry's death, planted many of their doctrines in the Anglican Church.

In Spain in the fifteenth and sixteenth centuries, religious persecution reached its greatest height. The Inquisition became a weapon of the state, and a succession of Spanish kings and queens tried to preserve peace and uphold national unity by stamping out heresy from the realm.

At this time a new Order was born which carried the Christian faith to the far corners of the earth. Ignatius Loyola, a Spaniard of noble birth, was so seriously wounded in battle that he was forced to leave the army. In the course of a long and painful convalescence he resolved to transfer his allegiance from the Spanish Crown to the service of Christ. In 1540, he founded the Society of Jesus, the Jesuit Order, to defend Christianity against all enemies. Every Jesuit was a soldier of Christ, subject only to the command of the Pope. Ignatius recruited scholars and saints to his cause, and the Order soon became a powerful influence in Catholic education and the most fearless and impressive missionary force in the world.

In the middle of the seventeenth century, armed religious conflict died down in Europe. The followers of Huss had been wiped out by severe persecution and Bohemia had become a stronghold of the Jesuit Order. Clergy in Luther's home province of Saxony and in other north German provinces established Lutheran churches; and Lutheran doctrine penetrated peacefully to Sweden, Norway, Denmark, and Finland. Calvin's followers had established Reformed churches in many Swiss cantons, lands along the Rhine known as the Palatinate, and in Holland. John Knox, a Scottish divine who had worked with Calvin, carried his faith to Scotland where it took firm root under the name of the Presbyterian Church. France was divided between Huguenot and Roman Catholic communities. Italy, Spain, Austria, and almost all Ireland remained true to Rome, and the religious shape of Europe has changed very little since that day.

The term Protestant was used in its broadest sense to describe people, no matter what their nationality, who had declared their independence from the Church of Rome. The Protestants were divided among themselves into separate Churches and sects, each one conducting services in the native language of the congregation. Until very recently the Roman Catholic Church continued to use Latin.

The Lutheran Church clung closely to the principles of its founder, holding high his banner of perfect faith. The Presbyterian Church became the national Church of Scotland, governed in the early days by a stern but idealistic creed. The ministers and elders were respected, but also greatly feared by the community, for they confronted evildoers with the horrors of hell-fire and gave them little hope of redemption. Both the Scottish kirks, or churches, and the services held in them were extremely simple, and Sunday was a day of unrelieved solemnity. Even Calvin in his desire to establish absolute purity throughout the Church had not imposed such severe restrictions on his congregation. Gradually, however, the Presbyterians have softened their laws and broadened their outlook, without at the same time lowering their moral standard. At the time of the Reformation new continents were being opened up and soon Scotsmen began to emigrate. Wherever they settled, they built churches and brought their children up in the Presbyterian faith.

Subjected to the direction of the ruling sovereign and the English Parliament, the Church of England sought a middle course between the lavish ceremonial of the Roman Catholic Church and the austerity of the extreme reformers. Once the Church of England was established, Thirty-nine Articles of belief laid down, and a Book of Common Prayer compiled, all loyal subjects were expected to uphold the religion of the state. Most people were prepared to conform, but there remained a small persecuted Roman Catholic minority, and some religious rebels among the people who could not accept all the official doctrines. They were ardent Christians but passionate individualists.

They formed groups—the Presbyterians, Congregationalists, Baptists, Quakers, and many others—and founded Free Churches. These nonconformists had a profound effect on the spread of Western Christianity and on the history of the United States of America.

The Roman Catholic is by far the largest Church in Christendom. It has over five hundred million members, more than all the other Christian Churches combined. Roman Catholics are a very united body, bound together by the absolute belief that theirs is the only true Church, with Christ its invisible head in Heaven and the Pope its visible head on earth. They accept the Pope's sovereignty with unquestioning obedience, confident that as the chosen successor to St. Peter, his official pronouncements are certain to be just and wise.

The Roman Catholic and Eastern Orthodox Churches have each preserved their own elaborate ritual and brilliant pageantry, their many altar candles, their incense, and the holy relics of their saints. They recognize seven sacraments as channels of divine grace between God and man: baptism, when the human body enters into Christ; confirmation when Catholic children confirm their membership of the Church; confession and penance to restore the union with God damaged or broken by sin; marriage which seeks the blessing of God for family life; extreme unction when a priest anoints with oil those on the verge of death; holy orders which create the institution of priesthood; and the most sublime and mysterious experience of all, the Holy Eucharist, or mass, when they believe that the actual body of Christ is offered and received in the form of bread and wine.

Protestants stress only the two sacraments of baptism and the Holy Eucharist as necessary for all Christians. They regard the bread and wine in Holy Communion as the outward and visible signs by means of which they receive the power of Christ's risen life.

Christian churches vary in grandeur from great cathedrals to humble meetinghouses. All Catholic and many Protestant churches are adorned with pictures and statues of Christ, of the Virgin Mary, and of patron saints. Because devout Catholics bestow even deeper adoration on the Virgin than Protestants, she is represented more often in their churches and their homes. In

An Anglican christening

the Eastern Orthodox churches statues are forbidden and painted icons take their place. Confession is rarely heard in Protestant churches, but in other Christian communities it is an essential part of religious life. The priests sit at appointed times in confessional boxes in the main body of the church and receive the penitents.

Church discipline for Catholics is stricter and more far-reaching than for Protestants. They must attend mass every Sunday if it is physically possible. They must conscientiously observe the fasts of the Catholic calendar. If either the father or mother of a family is a Catholic, the children must be brought up in the Catholic faith. Divorce is not permitted in any circumstances whatsoever, and parents may not limit the size of their families by artificial means. Most Protestant ministers recognize the need for divorce in cases of great unhappiness and a few permit remarriage. They do not lay down the laws of intimate family life.

Perhaps the most striking difference in the religious rules of the Christian Churches appears in the marriage laws of the clergy. In the early days of Christianity many priests had wives and children, but in the fourth century the Pope decreed that men who had a religious calling must remain celibate, or unmarried. When they took Holy Orders, they dedicated their whole lives to God and promised him their undivided service. The ruling senates of the Eastern Churches, on the other hand, decreed that married men could become priests, though they forbade them to marry once they were ordained, and elected only unmarried clergy as bishops. Protestants have gone further.

They welcome married men into the ministry, encourage men who are already ministers to marry if they wish to, and promote them to the highest positions in the Church.

Members of the Roman Catholic Church consider that their priests have more to offer their parishioners because they have renounced the ties of family life. Members of the Protestant and Eastern Orthodox Churches, however, feel most strongly that their priests are more understanding because they are husbands and fathers.

Saints' days vary from country to country, but the festivals and fasts of the early Christian Church are still observed throughout Christendom and Sunday is a day of worship and rest. Christmas, or Christ Mass, joyously commemorates the birth of Jesus; the forty days of Lent, ending at Easter, are set aside as a period of self-restraint and prayer in memory of Jesus' hardship in the wilderness. Good Friday, in memory of Christ's death, is the most somber day of the Christian year; but two days later on Easter Sunday Christians celebrate with wonder and gladness the miracle of the Resurrection.

Despite the centuries of bloodshed, bitterness, and suspicion which divided the Christian Church the inner faith of practicing Christians all over the world is very similar. It is based on belief in the love of one God for man and the love of man for one God.

In 1948, Protestant clergy formed the World Council of Churches. It is a Christian fellowship composed of nearly two hundred Churches which meets at about five-year intervals. The Roman Catholic Church does not take part in this ecumenical

Roman Catholic nuns in America today

movement, but the Orthodox Churches of Greece, Russia, Bulgaria, and Poland have become members. Representatives of Anglican, Lutheran, Reformed, Congregationalist, Baptist, Quaker, Methodist, and many other Churches work for unity and renewed strength, and pray for mutual understanding.

In 1958, a new Pope, John XXIII, was elected by the College of Cardinals, and the gulf between the Roman Catholic Church and other Christian bodies was narrowed by the leadership of a great man. Pope John was the son of an Italian peasant, and he rose to high office through his extraordinary holiness and humanity. He transformed the Vatican, the Papal State in the center of Rome, from a shrine where pilgrims went to pay formal homage to a meeting place where they found inspiration and wisdom, humor and comfort. Pope John promoted good will and understanding among men of many creeds, and when he died in 1963 there was widespread sorrow.

The next Pope, Paul VI, has also worked for Christian unity. Soon after his election, he broke away from established tradition and set out on a pilgrimage to the Holy Land. No Pope had left Italy for a hundred and fifty years, but in January 1964, Pope Paul flew from Rome in an aircraft emblazoned with the Papal arms and bearing the gold and white colors of the Vatican. In Jerusalem the Pope celebrated mass in the Church of the Holy Sepulcher, and he received the aged Patriarch Athenagoras, head of the Eastern Orthodox Church, who had traveled from Istanbul, formerly Constantinople, to greet him. It was a historic event, for the treacherous conduct of the Church of Rome in the Fourth Crusade had left behind deep resentment and Pope and Patriarch had not met for five hundred years.

In October, 1965, Pope Paul made a one-day visit to New York, bearing a message to all mankind. In the General Assembly of the United Nations, he spoke for the world to hear and made a moving appeal for universal peace. Men and women of more than a hundred nations and many different creeds were uplifted by his presence and inspired by his words.

In March, 1966, an event occurred symbolic of the growing desire throughout the world for Christian unity. Dr. Ramsey, Archbishop of Canterbury, the See founded by St. Augustine and now the center of all the Anglican Churches, traveled to visit Pope Paul, the head of the Roman Catholic Church. An official visit of this kind had not taken place since 1534. Within the Vatican, before the altar of the famous Sistine Chapel, under a great painting of the Last Judgment, the two high prelates exchanged a solemn kiss of peace. The following day, in a joint declaration, they pledged their faith in Christian fellowship between the Roman Catholic Church and the Churches of the Anglican Communion. They affirmed their resolve for closer collaboration and promised to strive together for the solution of the serious problems that face the Christian Churches in the world today.

Since the foundation of Christendom, people have outwardly declared their reverence and faith by the high standard of their religious art. The cathedrals, churches, monasteries, and shrines that have arisen century after century display reverence for God through the highest genius of man, and their beauty has been a source of wonder and pride to countless generations.

At the end of the Second World War, thousands of European cities, towns, and villages lay in ruins; homes were wrecked and sacred buildings damaged or destroyed. In the following years, people began to repair the desecration of total war. Many cathedrals and churches have been restored to their former glory and others rebuilt according to their original designs.

At the same time exciting new cathedrals and churches have been built in twentieth-century style. The post-war world has witnessed revolutionary changes in religious art and modern architects have moved far away from traditional forms. In brick and marble, glass and stone, steel and concrete, they have planned and created centers of worship symbolic of the spirit of a new age, and they stand today, vivid expressions of contemporary faith.

13 · *Judaism in Many Lands*

THE TRAGIC NEWS of the destruction of the
Jewish Temple in Jerusalem in A.D. 70 traveled swiftly through
the Mediterranean world, filling every Jewish home with horror
and dismay. Though by this time many Jews had settled in
distant cities, they all looked back to Jerusalem as the heart of
the nation of Israel and the citadel of the Jewish faith. Its loss
was a crushing blow, but fortunately there were among the
leaders of Judaism men determined to defend their faith against
Roman conquest or any other peril.

In the two centuries before the birth of Christ, a difference
of opinion had arisen in the Jewish priesthood, and two religious
parties, the Pharisees and the Sadducees, emerged from the conflict. Both believed fervently in the divine guidance of the Torah,
but differed in the interpretation of its message. The leading
Pharisees were learned men from the common people, mainly
rabbis, a Hebrew word which means "teachers," or "masters."
They regarded Judaism as a universal and living faith, and ex-
plained its teaching in such a way that ordinary people could
apply it to everyday life.

The leading Sadducees, on the other hand, were of noble birth, princely priests who administered the Temple and attended to matters of ritual. Their whole existence was so closely bound up with the Temple that their influence did not outlive its destruction. The Pharisees had a wider outlook, so they were able to withstand the loss of the Temple and to plan for the survival of their faith. The rabbis set out to preserve Hebrew wisdom and promote the way of life they believed in. They gathered around them little bands of devout and scholarly Jews to examine the holy scriptures and expound Jewish tradition. From these studies the rabbis collected a great store of knowledge and set it down in the volumes of the Talmud, a collection of writings which became almost as sacred as the Torah. The Talmud is a record of learned discussions on Jewish law and a detached statement of Jewish belief. It embodies the essence of the spirit of the Jewish people. Possession of the Talmud has bound them together against countless odds.

After their dispersal, the Jews lived in exile but they continued to regard Jerusalem as their rightful capital. The site that Solomon had chosen was forever hallowed. There is an old Jewish saying: "God measured all cities and found only Jerusalem worthy to have the Temple." Therefore they did not try to build another temple anywhere else. Instead, groups of exiled Jews met on the Sabbath at the house of a rabbi and combined worship with religious instruction. Prayer meetings had already been an established part of Jewish life since the return from the exile in Babylon. These meetings grew into the synagogues, which increased in number through the centuries and are active centers of Judaism today. The word synagogue is a Greek one which originally meant "an assembly" and came to mean "a building."

All over the world Jewish people built synagogues following the architectural style of whichever country they were living in. The interiors are usually simple and always dignified in design. The walls are bare of pictures or statues, and in the place of an altar there stands the most sacred symbol of Jewish faith, the Ark containing parchment scrolls on which the Torah is inscribed in Hebrew. At almost all services sections of the Torah are read aloud. The Ark has many forms, ranging from a simple wooden box to a recess with richly decorated doors. When the doors are opened, the scrolls are revealed to the congregation, sometimes encased in velvet, fringed with gold, and crowned with silver ornaments. The Ark is usually built so that when the worshipers turn reverently toward it in solemn prayer, they face in the direction of Jerusalem.

In the United States, there are three groups within Judaism: Orthodox, Conservative, and Reform. Orthodox Jews lay great stress upon Jewish laws and traditions, and believe that they should not be changed except by high authority in extreme circumstances. They would prefer to alter the times to suit the laws rather than alter the laws to suit the times. In Orthodox Judaism, synagogue services are conducted in Hebrew, and men and women sit in separate sections of the sanctuary.

Conservative Jews for the most part are more lenient in the matter of Jewish laws and traditions. They believe in their importance, but feel that it is right to adapt some of the most antiquated to meet the contemporary needs of the people. In

The scrolls of the Torah

Conservative Judaism, synagogue services are conducted in both Hebrew and English, and men and women are not separated.

Reform Jews generally do not consider ancient Jewish laws to be meaningful to them. But they lay great stress on the moral teachings of the prophets. They hold their services in English, with families sitting together.

Though they differ in their approach to Judaism, Orthodox, Conservative, and Reform Jews are conscious that they are all one people, bound together by a common heritage and history.

Judaism is deeply concerned with daily living and social service. The synagogues are designed as bases for friendly gatherings, welfare work, and education, as well as for prayer. People bring their joys and sorrows, their problems and successes, to share them with their neighbors.

There is a marked contrast in the organization of different synagogues. Some consist merely of a gathering of Jews who conduct their own services. Other wealthier and better established communities appoint rabbis and cantors to conduct the services and special readers to chant from the Torah. The rabbis are the preachers and teachers of their communities and they are almost always married men.

Second only to the synagogue in holiness is the Jewish home. Family life is consecrated to God, and traditional Jewish families are usually very united. They are bound together by affection and discipline. As soon as children can speak they are taught to recite certain verses of the Torah. It is just a part of growing up. When they can read, they learn long passages by heart, especially the revealed law contained in the first five books of the Torah, which are particularly sacred. Circumcision, confirmation, and marriage are carried out according to ancient custom. A Jewish bridegroom turns to his bride and says to her, "Behold thou are sanctified to me by this ring according to the Law of Moses and Israel." The Talmud contains rules for every aspect of life, and children grow up with the guidance of Jewish doctrine in whatever they do.

Every Jewish festival is a family occasion. The weekly Sab-

The festival of the Passover

bath falls on a Saturday, and it is a day of rest and rejoicing. On the festival of the Passover, the Jewish people give thanks for their deliverance from bondage in Egypt. The Passover celebrations last for eight days, and they begin with a service at home known as the *seder*. The opening words are spoken by the youngest child, who puts four traditional questions to the senior member of the family. The first of these questions is, "Why is this night different from all other nights?" During the *seder* the family recites together the story of the deliverance from bondage. During the whole period of the Passover, Jews eat ritual food, prepared and served on dishes kept for this special purpose according to ancient custom. Because the Children of Egypt fled from Egypt so hurriedly, they had no time to bake bread. Instead, they baked the dough before it had risen; so during Passover their descendants eat unleavened bread in memory of that historical event.

On the feast of Sukkoth, many traditional Jews still set up booths or huts in their gardens or on their balconies, and spend the week out of doors, as they did in ancient days. A period of great solemnity is the ten days between the Jewish New Year, Rosh ha-Shanah, and Yom Kippur, the Day of Atonement, the holiest day in the Jewish calendar. It is a time of reflection and prayer to ask God for help and forgiveness.

After the destruction of the Second Temple in A.D. 70, the Jews of the dispersal made their way at first to cities in Persia, Arabia, Syria, and Egypt, where they formed closely knit groups with people of their own faith. Most of these cities were already populated by Arab, Greek, African, and Hebrew communities, each speaking their own language, practicing their own religion, and occupying separate districts. As Christianity spread through the Middle East, it became a dominating influence and it mattered more what a man believed in than where he came from. With the advent of Mohammed the balance of religious power in the Middle East changed with dramatic suddenness and the boundaries of Christianity shrank. The Jews, who had no kingdom to lose, suffered less from the rise of Islam than the Christian subjects of the Byzantine Empire.

Gradually, enterprising Jewish merchants began to explore markets in the European countries. They settled in Italy, France, and Germany, crossed the sea to Britain, and traveled eastward to Poland and Russia. Many went to Spain where they met with stern oppression from Visigothic rulers who had turned from paganism to Christianity. When, in the eighth century, the armies of Islam entered Spain the Jews welcomed them as friends and liberators and together Jew and Moslem enjoyed a golden age of prosperity and religious toleration rare in Jewish history. It lasted almost five hundred years, until the Spanish Inquisition exiled every Jew who would not turn Christian.

As the Christian Church grew stronger, Jewish communities suffered from violent outbursts of persecution. The feeling behind these attacks is known today as anti-Semitism, and it arose from several different causes. Foremost among them in Christian and Islamic countries was religious prejudice. People felt that the Jews were an alien influence, liable to introduce new ideas and lead members of other faiths astray. In addition to this fear of heresy, the inhabitants of European and Asian towns and cities resented the fact that the Jews kept to themselves. Though they settled in certain countries for generations, they remained apart, preserving their age-old faith intact.

Though many Jewish people are talented and thrifty, industrious and able, their opportunities for advancement have been, until the nineteenth century, very limited. Christian law did not allow them to employ slaves at a time when slave labor was almost universal, and it prevented them from owning land so that it was impossible for them to make a living from farming.

So Jews congregated in towns and cities looking for work. But once more they were handicapped because the Christian guilds which taught skills and organized business would not enroll Jewish members. Many able Jews were therefore forced to turn to finance and did very well. They dealt in gold instead of goods, and became bankers and moneylenders.

In the fourteenth century, Yiddish began to be the common language of world Jewry. It developed first as a blend of Hebrew and German, and later, as Jews moved into Eastern Europe, absorbed elements of Slavonic dialects. By means of Yiddish, Jews built up a network of world-wide communications, one of the forerunners of international banking. Kings and princes recognized their usefulness and employed them to collect taxes, manage affairs of state, and raise money to pay for wars.

Men in other trades grew jealous and resentful. But though Jewish financiers served their masters faithfully and well, they never gained personal security. When they first arrived in Christian and Moslem cities, they chose to live apart, built their synagogues, and brought up their children in the traditional way of life. As public opinion turned against the Jews, they were segregated by law in ghettos, or Jewish districts, surrounded by walls and locked in at night. They were deprived of legal rights and ordered to wear special yellow badges, Stars of David, to distinguish them from the rest of the population.

The first instance of organized persecution on a large scale took place during the First Crusade. Christian soldiers were roused to savage fury by agitators who told them that before they risked their lives in foreign lands they should exterminate unbelievers at home. At first in France, and then with increasing savagery as they marched through Germany, the crusaders attacked helpless Jewish families, dragged them into the streets, and when they steadfastly refused to renounce their religion, murdered them in cold blood. Many Jews who were forcibly baptized strangled their children lest a similar fate should befall them and then killed themselves rather than submit to the Christian Church. These massacres, or *pogroms*, marked a tragic turning point in Christian-Jewish relations. Formerly there had been instances of misunderstanding and suspicion, but outright violence was uncommon. After the First Crusade tolerance and friendship between Jew and Gentile were exceptional.

Wherever Jews settled they were always a minority, outnumbered by people of other faiths. Again and again they found themselves used as scapegoats and blamed for disasters over which they had no possible control. In 1349, the Black Death struck Europe, probably carried by traveling merchants from the East. In the dirt and lack of hygiene of medieval cities the plague spread like wildfire, and it is estimated that in two years a quarter of the entire population of Europe died. In a wild panic of hysterical fear, bands of Christians slaughtered whole Jewish communities whom they accused of spreading the plague to destroy the Church of Rome. As cleanliness plays an important part in Jewish religious discipline, conditions in the ghettos were generally better than those in the Christian quarters of the same cities, and the death rate from disease was not so high.

This comparative immunity made the Jews more suspect than ever and they had no way of proving that they did not protect themselves against the plague by witchcraft.

When the Christian Church set up the apparatus of the Inquisition, the position of European Jews grew suddenly even more dangerous. Christian bishops and priests used every means within their power to convert the Jews, for according to the law of the Roman Church it was only as Christians that they could be accused of heresy. In theory, if Jews remained true to their faith the courts of the Inquisition could not touch them. In actual fact most practicing Jews lived in constant fear of having all their property confiscated and spending the rest of their lives in penniless exile. From the time of the dispersal in A.D. 70 until the nineteenth century, Jews were inhabitants of many countries but citizens of none. Ruling sovereigns held direct power over the Jewish people in their realms and denied them the rights of ordinary citizens.

In Russia under the czars Jewish people fared very badly indeed. They were severely repressed by the Russian Orthodox Church and barred from the main cities by the state. Poverty-stricken families lived in overcrowded ghettos, walled into sternly restricted areas. With the coming of Communism and the decline in the influence of the Orthodox Church, the lot of Russian Jewry has slightly improved. But the most fortunate are those who left the country to make their lives in the New World of the West.

The fate of Jewish people in Western Europe in the centuries after the Reformation varied from country to country.

Reciting Hebrew texts

They won citizenship and emancipation slowly and painfully by their brains and ability, and by the determined effort of a few outstanding defenders of human rights. The nineteenth century was an era of revolution and reform. With widening education the old-established evils of slavery and child labor were abolished. Downtrodden people in many lands began to demand an equality and freedom which they had never dreamed of before.

One by one European nations granted full rights of citizenship to the Jews living in their territories. For the first time since they were driven out of Jerusalem, Jewish men and women were able to take their rightful place among the countrymen of their adopted lands. When the doors of opportunity were opened to Jewish enterprise and creative spirit, it became clear that centuries of persecution had completely failed to dim the faith, blot out the genius, or quench the basic energy of the Jewish people. In the last hundred years Jewish men and women have risen to the highest ranks of their professions and excelled as scholars and scientists, doctors and lawyers, painters and musicians, actors and poets. They have enriched the world with their attainments.

In the second half of the nineteenth century, thousands of Jews escaped from political unrest in Germany and Eastern Europe, and crossed the Atlantic to settle in America. They had little money but a capacity for hard work and a desperate need to make good. Many of them had left their families behind, promising to send for them as soon as they could pay the passage. These immigrants entered a continent which had high ideals of liberty and no tradition of ghettos. In 1787, the Constitutional Convention of the United States declared that "no religious test shall ever be required as a qualification to any office or public trust." Jews found to their astonishment that they were not penalized for their faith. In due course they applied for citizenship, and it was granted. They swore to serve their adopted country faithfully, and shared a nationality and a flag on equal terms with other Americans. They could go to college, own land, and vote in elections.

Suddenly, all over the world Jews found that they possessed a strength outside their religion, but that in return they were expected to obey laws which were not set down in the Torah. Instead of being simply Jewish, they were nationals of America, Britain, France, Germany, Italy, and many other countries. Because they had new allegiances, they were not so dependent on each other. They began to develop new interests, drift away from the synagogues, and reject traditional ties.

Already in Germany, during the nineteenth century, some Jewish leaders had been trying to introduce reforms into Judaism which would hold Jews true to their faith but make it easier for them to live in harmony with their countrymen. They tried to combine the finest features of Jewish law with the spirit of a modern age.

Reform Judaism emerged from this religious search. It attracted many followers, particularly in Western Europe and the United States, but there are still large Jewish communities which observe the ancient rituals and accept the inflexible discipline of Orthodox Judaism. Rabbis of Reform Judaism have accepted certain changes in traditional ritual. They are growing more liberal in their outlook and conduct services in the language of whatever country they live in instead of always in Hebrew. They have decided it is wise to adapt many of the Sabbath rules to fit the pattern of Western life.

By the twentieth century, most Jews had become loyal and respected citizens of the countries where their ancestors had lived in fear and insecurity. In Germany especially they played a leading role in business, art, and science. They fought in the armed forces and served in the government. In 1918, at the end of the First World War, Germany had been severely defeated and she was no longer a great power. The German people were sunk in the depths of despair. Their pride was broken and they had no hope for the future. In the 1930's, a world depression spread from the United States to Europe, and the Germans suffered worst of all. Millions of men and women were out of work and starving.

At this time of sadness and suffering, a ruthless politician named Adolf Hitler, leader of the Nazi Party, became supreme dictator of Germany. He won the confidence of the German people by false promises and visions of greatness. They were hungry and he offered them food, downcast and he told them they were a master race. He worked them up into a frenzy of patriotic fervor, using the Jews as a target for mass hatred. Hitler blamed the Jewish people for Germany's defeat and all her other troubles. He swore to wipe out every Jew in a crusade for German revival. He won a following because many Germans were so desperate that they had lost all sense of humanity and justice. At the same time, Hitler's words sounded so fantastic to people in other countries that they could not take them seriously. Between 1933, when Hitler came to power, and 1945, when he committed suicide, six million defenseless Jews died from starvation, the strain of forced labor, or in vast concentration camps where gas chambers had been specially built for wholesale murder. It was a crime that has no equal in history.

It must always be remembered, however, in the records of the Hitler regime, that there were individual Germans who, revolted by the cruelty and injustice of Nazi policy, with immense courage risked torture and death to save the lives of Jewish families and help them to escape.

Through all the centuries of want and wandering after the dispersal, the Jewish people never wholly abandoned hope of returning to Palestine, the Promised Land of their forefathers. Many had made pilgrimages to sacred shrines in Jerusalem and lamented their cruel fate at the Wailing Wall, all that remained of the glory of the great Temple. But few had stayed to settle for the land was poor and mainly peopled by wandering Arab tribes, tending flocks of goats and raising scanty crops with primitive tools.

After their conquest of Constantinople in 1453, the Ottoman Turks ruled Palestine and large territories in Western Asia, until the end of the First World War when they were decisively defeated by the combined armies of Britain and her allies. By this time Palestine was a disputed area. Prominent American and British Jews had prepared a plan to found a new Jewish state there. They called themselves Zionists, and won support for their scheme from the British government and from wealthy influential Jews in the United States. The Arabs who occupied the country wished to rule it and stubbornly opposed the Zionist scheme.

The state of Israel

In 1922, Palestine was declared a British Mandate and placed in the care of the British Government until a just solution could be found. When Hitler launched his merciless campaign, the suffering of the Jews aroused the anger and pity of the civilized world. To many people it seemed only right that homeless refugees should have a chance to rebuild their lives in the country they had once called their own.

For the first time, the partition of Palestine between Arabs and Jews was openly discussed. But there was no meeting ground between them, violent fighting broke out, and finally, in desperation, the British handed the problem to the United Nations. After heated debate, a majority of nations in the General Assembly voted for partition in spite of bitter opposition from every Arab country. The dividing lines were drawn, and in May 1948 the Jewish people triumphantly proclaimed a new nation under the ancient name of Israel.

Statistics show that in 1964 there were about twelve million Jews in the world. Half of them lived in the United States, two million in Russia, and just over two million in Israel. Their survival as a distinct people is one of the most remarkable facts in the history of mankind. Now in Israel a new chapter of Jewish history is being written year by year.

Through the ages, in scattered communities, the Jewish people have continued to pray for the coming of the Messiah. The expectation of an answer to this prayer has never left them, and it has bound them together. Some Jews see in the new state of Israel the fulfillment of prophesy and some an epic of patriotic endeavor. There is no doubt that it is a severe test of courage, for hostile Arabs occupy the surrounding countries. They resent a Jewish nation in their midst and have sworn to destroy it. Since 1948, more than a million Jewish immigrants have arrived in Israel passionately resolved to defend their frontiers. They came from Eastern and Western Europe, the Americas, and the Moslem countries of the Middle East. They arrived speaking seventy different languages and holding conflicting political opinions. They dressed, worked, and thought in entirely different ways. But they shared four thousand years of past history and an intense longing to build an imperishable Jewish state for future generations.

In Israel today Hebrew has been revived as a common language. Though Judaism is the dominant religion, Moslems and Christians are free to worship as they wish, and teachers are trying to shape a society built on freedom, equality, tolerance, mutual help, and love of mankind.

In general Jews are very proud of their new nation, but Judaism is a world religion much wider than any particular country. The bonds which hold the Jewish people together are woven of age-old religious tradition rather than of current support and sympathy for Israel.

14 · *Christians Conquer the New World*

THE RECORDED HISTORY of the New World begins in 1492 when Christopher Columbus, an Italian sea captain, sailing under the Spanish flag, crossed the Atlantic and discovered islands which he named the West Indies, because he did not realize the American continent existed and imagined he had reached the west coast of Asia. He was followed by other European explorers who sailed further and landed on the mainland. In little more than a hundred years, white men conquered the whole area now known as Latin America and imposed their rule and religion on the inhabitants. European rule lasted until the nineteenth century and Christianity is the prevailing faith there today.

When Europeans first set foot on American shores the continent was populated by hundreds of Asian tribes who, it is supposed, crossed the narrow Bering Strait which separates what are now Russian Siberia and the American state of Alaska. Since the earliest white settlers thought, like Columbus, that they were in India, they called these people Indians, and because of their bronze coloring, nicknamed them "redskins."

For countless centuries, fresh migrations of American Indians must have arrived and fanned out to the east and trekked southward until they reached Cape Horn more than ten thousand miles away. It seems that they entered an empty land and developed ways of life to fit the climate and resources of the regions they occupied. They were skilled hunters and practical farmers. They hunted herds of buffalo in the north, and raised llamas and vicuñas in the south, ate their meat and wore their skins. By the end of the fifteenth century two strong tribes, the Aztecs in Mexico and the Incas in Peru, had discovered gold and built powerful empires. The rulers and nobles lived in barbaric splendor, but they lacked two essentials of civilization, for they had not invented wheeled vehicles nor any form of writing.

Historians have not been able to decide how many million Indians populated the American continent before the European conquest, but there were certainly hundreds of tribes and clans and many different languages. It is evident that their numbers have sadly diminished, particularly in North America. Some tribes suffered so badly from wars against white men and the loss of their lands that they died out altogether. The Canadian and United States Governments have recently set aside territory, and built schools and hospitals, to care for the Eskimos in the north and pockets of Indians scattered through the two countries. But it is hard for these people who are used to living in the wilds to adapt themselves to an industrial age and take their place in a modern society. In 1960, out of a total North

American population of about a hundred and eighty million, less than a million were Indian born.

Most Indians have been converted to Christianity but formerly their religious customs varied from clan to clan and tribe to tribe. Many of them worshiped one almighty power, a supreme Creator, a Great Spirit, a sun god or an earth goddess. The Aztecs offered up human sacrifices to win the favor of the gods and gain divine protection. Life was violent and insecure and most Indian religions were mainly concerned with winning wars, obtaining food, and curing disease. Every tribe had medicine men who wove magic spells and conducted tribal ceremonies with music and ritual dances. Each tribe had its traditional festival costumes of woven cloth, hides, fur, feathers, and colored beads. They were works of native art, treasured possessions, handed down from generation to generation. In certain tribes young warriors, or braves, willingly endured an ordeal of long-drawn-out physical torture, suffering indescribable agony to prove themselves worthy to receive the Great Spirit.

Some North American Indian clans practiced the cult of Totemism which exists also among the aborigines, the original inhabitants of Australia. It is a form of worship based on a magic association of a group of people with a group of animals, birds, or fishes. Often the members of a totemic tribe believed that their ancestors were bears, wolves, eagles, or eels, and these creatures must never be killed or eaten on that account.

Impelled by territorial ambition and religious fervor, Spanish pioneers played the leading part in discovering and conquering the New World. In 1492, the Battle of Granada put an end to nearly eight centuries of Moorish occupation, and Spain was united under King Ferdinand of Aragon and Queen Isabella of Castile. These Catholic sovereigns decided that religious unity was an essential foundation for a strong nation, and that their subjects could only be good Spaniards if they were also true Catholics. They adopted the Inquisition as a weapon of state.

It is easy after four hundred years have passed to condemn this religious persecution as both cruel and senseless, but at the time it was an expression of faith and patriotism which won the support of a number of sincere though overzealous men who had the love of the Church and the prosperity of Spain at heart. Spanish priests were consumed by a burning desire to rescue Moslems, Jews, and dissenting Christians from the perils of misbelief and shelter them within the fold of the true faith; and Spanish statesmen feared that religious differences would lead to fresh outbreaks of war.

As the relentless machinery of the Inquisition went into action, Moslems and Jews, deeply integrated in the economic and cultural life of Spain, were converted, imprisoned, exiled, or burned at the stake. Even those who became Christians never outlived the reputation of having been born in another faith. The outcome was disastrous for oppressors and oppressed. The victims of the Inquisition were either martyred or expelled from the country, and Spain never recovered from the loss of their talent and industry.

In the midst of this religious ferment, Christopher Columbus persuaded Queen Isabella to finance his first voyage of discovery. He set out with three small ships and boundless courage. When he returned in triumph the following year, bringing a few Indian captives and a little gold, the news spread swiftly and stirred the imagination of all kinds and conditions of men. Kings and princes dreamed of a mighty overseas empire; fortune seekers conjured up visions of untold treasure; and Catholic clergy, fired with missionary ardor, prayed for a rich harvest of pagan souls.

From this time onward, a succession of explorers crossed the Atlantic and few ships set sail without a priest aboard.

In 1519 Hernando Cortés, a Spanish adventurer and soldier of fortune, was dispatched to Mexico, to seize the land of the Aztecs. Cortés was remarkably brave, eager for gold, and ambitious to extend Spanish power. He set out with about five hundred and fifty men, some cannon, and twenty horses, to subdue Montezuma, the supreme ruler of the Aztec Empire, who had tens of thousands of warriors under his command.

Cortés landed on the shores of the Gulf of Mexico with his little army, founded the city of Vera Cruz, the True Cross, and built the first Christian church on the American continent. When he reached Tenochtitlan, the Aztec capital, he was excited to find that rumors of Aztec wealth were not exaggerated. The Spaniards admired the magnificent palaces and temples set in luxuriant gardens; but they viewed in horror a great temple-pyramid overshadowing all other buildings, and dedicated to the god of war. Grotesque serpent heads jutted from the tiered walls, and on the crest stood a stone altar, caked with the blood of human sacrifice.

Cortés knew that his meager force did not stand a chance in open battle against the Aztec armies. By trickery and daring he took Montezuma prisoner and enlisted rebel chieftains to fight against Aztec rule. The conflict was bloodthirsty and bitter, and it was two years before Cortés proclaimed Aztec territory the New Spain, raised his flag over the ruined capital, established Christian churches in pagan precincts, and opened the way to Mexican gold.

The conquest of the Inca empire of Peru came shortly afterward. It is an epic of valiant leadership and tragic betrayal, a mixture of triumph and shame. Inca territory extended for three thousand miles along the lofty chain of the Andes Mountains and the Pacific coastal strip beneath. It was a highly organized pagan state, reputed to be rich in gold, and ruled by King Atahualpa, reverently referred to by his subjects as the Inca. In 1530, Francisco Pizarro, an illiterate Spanish peasant who had emigrated to South America in search of adventure, won the support of the Spanish Crown, and recruited a band of about three hundred men to vanquish the Inca empire. He had spent his boyhood tending his father's pigs, and he had little to lose in Spain and everything to gain in Peru.

As Pizarro left the safety of the plain and headed for the mountains, deep into the heart of Inca country, he must have known the dangers ahead. Peru was a tempting prize, but it might well be that he was leading his men into a death trap with no escape from a pitiless and powerful enemy. The sol-

An Inca sacrificial site

diers too were probably filled with fear and foreboding as they threaded their way through the narrow defiles leading to the Inca's capital, but they pressed on.

It turned out, however, that Atahualpa was friendly. He came unarmed to meet the Spaniards, riding in a golden litter carried by his principal nobles, and attended by a retinue of thousands of his people. When the royal procession halted, Vicente Valverde, a Dominican friar and Pizarro's personal chaplain, approached Atahualpa with a crucifix in one hand and a Bible in the other, telling him through an interpreter that the Spaniards had come on a sacred mission to lead the Inca and his people into the ways of God. The king listened but was not convinced; he turned over the pages of the Bible and then cast it away. The Spaniards were horrified by this sacrilege, and suddenly, with blazing cannon and flashing swords, they attacked. The unarmed Incas fled in blind panic, but they could not escape and the Spanish soldiers mowed them down. Before night fell, five thousand Incas had been massacred, and Atahualpa captured. Only one Spaniard was injured.

Pizarro pledged his word to release the Inca in return for a room filled from floor to ceiling with treasure. Day after day the Incas came laden with gold and silver ornaments to redeem their king. When the tribute was melted down every soldier received a share and a "royal fifth" was set aside for the Spanish Crown.

But in the end Pizarro broke his promise. He dared not set the Inca free for fear he would take revenge on the Spanish army. Striving for a semblance of justice, Pizarro held a trial on trumped-up charges and sentenced the captive king to death. In his last hour Atahualpa renounced the faith of his forefathers and submitted to Christian baptism. In return he was spared the prolonged agony of being burned alive and was executed instead by the swifter process of strangulation.

Meanwhile a Portuguese explorer named Cabral had proclaimed the great territory of Brazil a Portuguese possession, and one by one the other Indian lands fell to Spanish conquest. By about 1580 the Indians were defeated, and the entire continent of Latin America was ruled by white men.

When European settlers began to develop the lands they

had won, they were seriously handicapped by shortage of manpower. White men died in the unaccustomed heat and Indians had to be driven to work for foreign masters who demanded cheap labor in West Indian sugar plantations, Mexican and Peruvian gold mines, and Brazilian coffee and cotton fields.

Portuguese traders had been importing African Negroes for some time as farm laborers, and in 1512 they signed a contract with the king of Spain to supply slaves for his overseas empire. Dutch and British merchants later joined the slave trade, and many professing Christians dulled their consciences and made huge profits from an undertaking which caused intense suffering to their fellow human beings. During the next three hundred years, millions of West African men and women were crammed into the holds of sailing ships, carried across the Atlantic, and sold to Spanish, Portuguese, and later, in North America, to English buyers. The treatment on the voyage was so inhuman and the conditions so unhealthy that a large proportion of the Negroes never lived to see the New World. But those who survived worked, first as slaves and then as free citizens, and made an important contribution to the progress of the American people.

The Christian conversion of Latin America went step by step with the military conquest. The first missionaries were friars of the Franciscan and Dominican Orders. The Franciscans ministered mainly to working people, while the more learned Dominicans approached the educated classes. After the foundation of the Society of Jesus in the sixteenth century, the Jesuits were foremost in missionary endeavor all over the world. Mili-

Planting the Cross in the New World

tant in the cause of Christ, zealous and unafraid, they carried
the gospel from Spain to every newly discovered land. No
journey was too hazardous, no mission too lonely, and no
opposition too great to dampen their ardor.

As the Reformation did not penetrate Spain and Portugal, the Protestant Church took no part in this missionary activity. Latin America was infused with the spirit of Roman Catholicism, obedient to the Pope, and subject, in a moderated degree, to the Inquisition.

Indian chiefs were powerless to resist Spanish pressure but many tribes readily accepted Christian doctrine because it had something in common with their traditional beliefs. Faith in one supreme power did not seem strange to them, and the Aztecs already practiced baptism with water and ritual confession and penance. They abandoned human sacrifice without too much reluctance, but it was far more difficult to persuade them to give up polygamy, for they loved their numerous wives and took a pride in large families.

Christian priests soon discovered that they baptized more Indians if they respected some ancient habits of worship. They built many new churches, but they also consecrated pagan temples and raised the Cross in places where the Indians were accustomed to meet for religious ceremonies. Monks and nuns welcomed people at mass, but did not forbid them to perform in their villages the ritual dances that had been part of their lives for untold generations. Many understanding confessors were well aware that timid Indian mothers made the sign of the Cross while at the same time they kept little household idols hidden away in case of desperate emergency.

The Roman Catholic Church in Latin America was first and foremost a defender of Indian rights. In the early days o

A Catholic priest on his rounds in the mo.

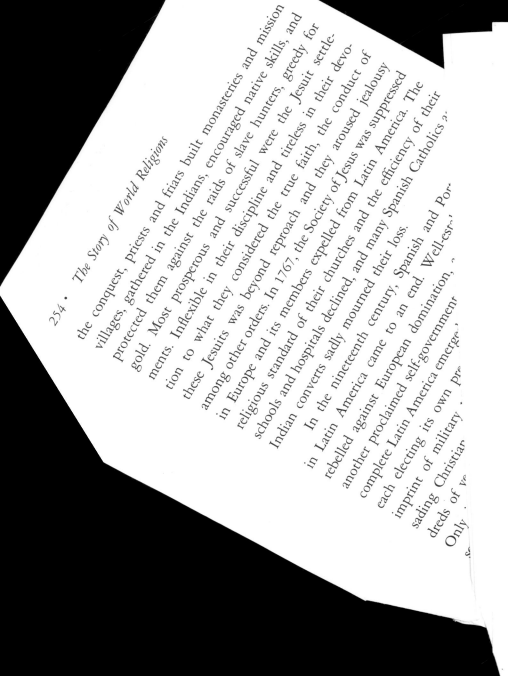

the conquest, priests and friars built monasteries and mission villages, gathered in the Indians, encouraged native skills, and protected them against the raids of slave hunters, greedy for gold. Most prosperous and successful were the Jesuit settlements. Inflexible in their discipline and tireless in their devotion to what they considered the true faith, the conduct of these Jesuits was beyond reproach and they aroused jealousy among other orders. In 1767, the Society of Jesus was suppressed in Europe and its members expelled from Latin America. The religious standard of their churches and the efficiency of their schools and hospitals declined, and many Spanish Catholics a̶ Indian converts sadly mourned their loss.

In the nineteenth century, Spanish and Por￰ in Latin America came to an end. Well-est￰ rebelled against European domination, ￰ another proclaimed self-government, ￰ complete Latin America emerg￰ each electing its own pr￰ imprint of military ￰ sading Christia￰ dreds of v￰ Only ￰

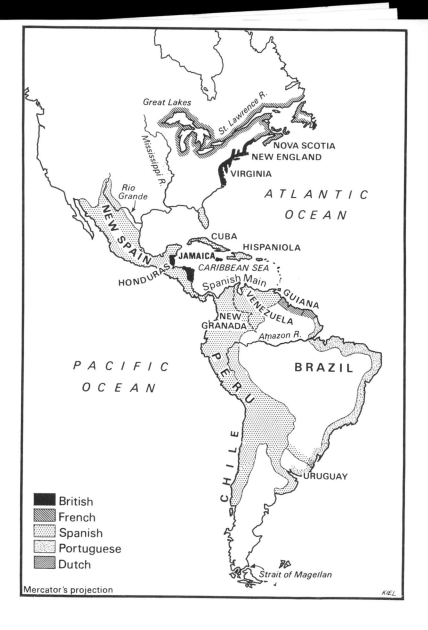

Christian settlement in the New World circa 1650

in horror from war or any kind of violence, and later they worked for social reform and the abolition of the slave trade. Quakers did not recognize class distinctions, clung to the old-fashioned "thee" and "thou" in conversation, and continued to wear the clothes of George Fox's day long after the fashions had changed. As dissenters, they were not admitted to many of the professions so they went into business where they put their theories on equality and justice into daily practice.

Small groups of Quakers emigrated to New England, but there they were more fiercely persecuted by the Puritans than by the Anglicans at home. In 1681 William Penn, a wise and worthy Quaker, founded a new colony named Pennsylvania, and built Philadelphia, the city of Brotherly Love. He established religious freedom and welcomed men of every faith. People flocked in from Europe, tired of war and eager to start fresh lives. Many of them were farmers and craftsmen, diligent and devout. They brought their skills and beliefs to the New World, determined to preserve them. Lutherans and members of the Reformed Churches came from Germany and Holland, and Huguenots from France. They were followed by a wave of Scotch-Irish Presbyterians, weavers who left Scotland for Northern Ireland to escape Anglican interference, and were thrown out of work when the English Parliament refused to buy Irish cloth. These Presbyterian Scots greatly influenced both the religious and political convictions of the American nation. They were hardy and freedom-loving, and they not only established churches but also played an important part in the struggle for independence. Pennsylvania prospered partly because, true to Quaker principles,

William Penn built up good relations with the neighboring Indian tribes, and avoided the wars that drained the resources of other colonies.

From within the Congregational Church there had arisen yet another sect, the Baptists, who differed from other Protestants mainly in their views on baptism. The Baptists originated on the European continent and arrived in England with other religious reformers. They did not lay down an official creed, for they believed that man's relationship with God needed no guidance from Church or state, no set articles to direct the pattern of worship, and no priests or preachers to uplift or depress the spirit. They still believe today that baptism should be carried out by total immersion in water, following the example of John the Baptist, and that no one should be baptized until they are old enough to decide for themselves whether they wish to make this public confession of Christian faith. In England, in the seventeenth century, the Baptists suffered from the same restrictions as other non-conformist sects. Many of them emigrated to America where they gathered a large following, particularly among the Negro slaves in the southern states, and eventually formed the largest Protestant community throughout the country. Unitarians also came to America and settled mainly in New England. They are Congregationalists who broke away from the main body of the Church because they believed in one absolute God and could not accept the conception of the Holy Trinity.

In the eighteenth century, the Methodist movement arose in England, inspired by the preaching of John Wesley. His father was an Anglican clergyman and his mother the daughter of a dissenting minister. John was fifteenth in a family of nineteen children, each one of whom received from their mother separate religious instruction every week. When he grew up he was ordained in the Anglican Church and soon afterwards set out for America to spread the gospel in Georgia. But the colonists and the Indians were not receptive, the mission was a failure, and Wesley returned to London dispirited.

There he received what he himself afterwards described as a rebirth. He was filled with the love of God and determined to share it with mankind. This was a time of great hardship for the English working people. The industrial revolution had drawn them to the towns where many of them lived in abject poverty and squalor. The Church of England was short of clergy and appeared indifferent to their plight.

John Wesley worked among these people, striving to improve their conditions and comfort them with the words of God. He traveled thousands of miles, always on horseback, to towns and villages in England, Scotland, Ireland, and Wales, preaching wherever he could collect a congregation. In the country he gave free rein to his horse while he read the Bible, ancient classics, and contemporary poetry. Anglican parsons closed their churches to him so he held meetings in churchyards, fields, and market places. He preached to miners at the pitheads and dockers on the wharves. Hooligans tried to break up the meetings and pelted him with stones and rotten eggs; but Wesley's composure defeated them.

He was not only an inspired preacher but also a magnificent organizer. With his brother Charles and their close friend George

Whitefield, he set up Christian societies and trained, first a band of preachers, and then a full-time ministry, to direct them. Everywhere he went, he spoke of victory over sin and Christian companionship. His life was so orderly, his work so methodical, and his followers so well regulated that people called them Methodists, first as a term of derision and later with respect. Methodist preachers went to America and started societies in Pennsylvania and other states. By the end of the eighteenth century there were Methodist churches in most British and American cities.

In 1783, after six years of revolutionary war, the American colonies won their independence from British rule. The new Constitution proclaimed the ideals of liberty, justice, and religious tolerance. It stated specifically that no government appointment should be subject to any form of religious discrimination. When the break with England came, the American Churches were divided in their loyalties. In general the Congregationalists, Baptists, and Presbyterians supported the demand for independence; the Methodists had arrived too recently to exert much influence; the Anglicans were pro-British and resisted separation from the mother country; and the Quakers, with their hatred of war, tried to stand aside from the conflict.

After the Declaration of Independence the new nation found itself bitterly divided on the rights and wrongs of slavery. The northern states condemned it; and the southern states, where Negro slaves were employed on the sugar, rice, and tobacco plantations, defended it. Most of the Churches were unable to take a united stand against the injustice of slavery because the

Modern Methodist church in Florida

views of their congregations varied with the locality. Only the Congregationalists who lived entirely in the North, and the Quakers, who had always striven for social equality, were whole-heartedly against it. In 1865, after four tragic years of civil war, the southern states were defeated and the slaves freed.

In England, in 1829, almost the last obstacles standing in the way of complete religious toleration disappeared. The Church of England remains today by far the largest religious body in the country, but Roman Catholics, Jews, and members of all the Free Churches have equal rights in every sphere of national life. The Presbyterian Church is firmly established as the Church of Scotland and the Welsh people have adopted a Presbyterian-Methodist Church which holds many of its services in the Welsh language and has a dedicated following.

The nineteenth century was an age of social reform and the beginning of a great Protestant missionary movement. From Europe and from all the English-speaking nations, men and women set out bearing the message of Christianity to pagan peoples in distant lands. Following the example of Catholic priests, these Protestant missionaries braved the dangers of travel and disease, hostility and suspicion. They lived among cannibals and head-hunters, and worked with medicine men and magicians, endeavoring to dispel ignorance and evil. They penetrated the interior of darkest Africa, braved the frozen reaches of the Arctic Circle, and suffered untold hardship from hunger, thirst, and disease in many lands. They established little Christian outposts in remote regions, on coral islands and volcanic rocks. Many disappeared leaving no trace and no account of their endeavors,

A Benedictine missionary in Africa

but others carried on and founded missions that have grown and multiplied.

By the middle of the nineteenth century, the states along the eastern seaboard of North America were well established, and Americans had begun to look westward seeking land for their families, wealth, and adventure. Gradually enterprising pioneers moved out of the settled areas into an unknown wilderness sparsely populated by Indian tribes. The Indians fiercely resisted the white man's invasion of their lands. In the wars that followed they were outnumbered and outfought until they lost their herds of buffalo and their hunting grounds. Some tribes sank to a vestige of their former strength and some disappeared altogether.

There were no churches on this moving frontier, but preachers rode with the pioneers. Most Congregationalists remained in the East, but Methodists, Presbyterians, and Baptists carried their faith to the West. Following Wesley's example circuit riders held meetings by camp fires and on wagon trails. They staged a religious revival, or Great Awakening, among people who had almost lost their beliefs in the raw life of the frontier, and others who had come to America as soldiers or fortune seekers and probably never had any. On the crest of mass emotion men and women were carried away by the meetings. In an atmosphere of intense excitement, they saw visions and answered the call with a lack of restraint which shocked the conventional ministers of the Anglican and Congregational Churches.

But these pioneer preachers played an important part in

the development of American life. Eventually they established churches throughout the length and breadth of the country. They brought together people of different backgrounds and enrolled them in the denomination of their choice. At first in lonely districts where families lived on widely separated holdings, and later in villages, towns, and cities, the church became the recognized meeting place and center of social life.

The religious pattern of the United States was first set by waves of immigration from Europe and Asia, and later reshaped by the movements of people within the country itself.

Today New England remains largely Congregational and Pennsylvania continues to be a Quaker and Presbyterian stronghold. There are more Methodists in the West than anywhere else in the country and more Baptists in the South. In the early 1960's, out of a total American population of one hundred and eighty million, over forty million were practicing Roman Catholics. Many of them came to the New World in the nineteenth century to escape the terrible potato famines in Ireland and mass unemployment in Italy, and found work in the eastern states. At the same time millions of Jews fled from oppression in Eastern Europe and later from the pitiless persecution of the Hitler regime, settled mainly in the large cities, and built their own synagogues. In Washington, D.C., a great cathedral stands as an expression of Episcopalian faith. It is designed to serve the American nation, a church for people of every state and all ages. Clergy of many religions hold services within its stately walls and in the simple beauty of a miniature chapel little children learn to pray.

The children's chapel in Washington Cathedral

In addition to the many shades of religious belief that originated in Europe or Asia, three separate Churches were born of the Christian faith and grew up on American soil.

The Disciples of Christ are proud to be typically American and they trace their ancestry and the foundation of their Church back to the challenging days of the moving frontier. Life was dangerous and congregations scattered, and the Disciples developed a simple faith, based on the teaching of the Presbyterian Church, which fulfilled their needs and brought them strength and comfort in the midst of a changing world. They respect the teaching of the New Testament and are above all Disciples of Christ as their title proudly proclaims.

The Church of Jesus Christ of Latter Day Saints, or the Mormon Church, was conceived in 1820 by Joseph Smith, a fifteen-year-old boy who lived in New York State, and saw in a vision the words of God engraved on tablets of gold. Joseph translated the tablets and gave them to his followers as the Book of Mormon. Then he led them westward, seeking a new Jerusalem. Because the Mormons thought it right to take more than one wife they were violently persecuted, and Joseph Smith was murdered. His successor, Brigham Young, gave the Mormons courage to endure the extreme hardships of a journey through Indian country, across the great plains and mountain ranges, until they reached the silver shores of a great lake where they founded Salt Lake City and built a stately temple. In 1890, they agreed to abandon polygamy, and Utah, the state where they live, was admitted to the Union. The Mormons are now a highly organized religious body, professing faith in God and giving their services and a regular share of their income to the community as a whole.

In the second half of the nineteenth century, Mary Baker Eddy founded the Church of Christ Scientist in Boston, Massachusetts. She believed that she had rediscovered Jesus' method of healing and that faith in God is the remedy for ills of the body and spirit. Christian Scientists study the Bible and base their life upon its teaching. They do not have ministers, but instead appoint practitioners to carry out the Church's work of healing. Christian Science has spread to many countries, bearing the message that good is immortal, evil a delusion, and that sin, death, and disease do not exist.

White men went to the New World to conquer and stayed to rule; black men went in chains and stayed to win their freedom. Many pioneers arrived with guns in their hands and some with greed in their hearts. But others had Bible teaching in their minds and the Cross before their eyes, and their followers have endeavored ever since to turn harshness into humanity and spread the principles of equality and justice.

Epilogue: Religion Today

RELIGIOUS BELIEF has been the inspiration and the driving force behind human thought and human action from time immemorial. Today religious leaders are facing a dangerous challenge. Material possessions have become increasingly important to a great many people and spiritual values tend to be cast aside.

The power of the Church is no longer absolute in any country, and religious persecution has almost disappeared. Therefore people worship of their own free will, or not at all. In every community there are agnostics, who question the existence of an almighty power and admit that they cannot find a satisfactory answer, and atheists, who have weighed up religious teaching and decided there is no God.

At the same time, in both Eastern and Western countries a great upsurge of religious conviction is finding an outlet in social service and missions of mercy. Young people and old are expressing their faith by defending the rights and promoting the welfare of mankind.

The story of world religions belongs to all of us, for every living person has some part in it. The more we learn about our own beliefs, the better we can understand the beliefs of other people. In the past, ecumenical, or world-wide, conferences were rare events; now, they are held all the time. Religious tolerance is a fine quality if it comes from knowledge and understanding; but it has no value if it arises from ignorance and indifference. There has never been an age when so many people gave so much thought to the matter of their beliefs and studied with such interest and excitement the foundations of their faith.

Bibliography

Comparative Religion   A. C. Bouquet. (Pelican) Penguin Books, Inc.,
   1950.
A Short History of Religions   E. E. Kellett. (Pelican) Penguin Books,
   Inc., 1963.
Oriental Religions in Roman Paganism   Franz Cumont. Peter Smith.
   (Paperback) Dover Publications, Inc.
World Religions and World Community   Robert H. L. Slater. Columbia
   University Press, 1963.
Orpheus, a History of Religions   Solomon Reinach. Liveright Publishing
   Corp. and Tudor Publishing Co., 1932.
A Historian's Approach to Religion   Arnold Toynbee. Oxford University
   Press, Inc., 1956.
The Story of Civilization   Will Durant. Simon and Schuster, Inc.
   1. *Our Oriental Heritage,* 1935.
   2. *The Life of Greece,* 1939.
   3. *Caesar and Christ,* 1944.
   4. *The Age of Faith,* 1950.
   5. *The Renaissance,* 1953.
   6. *The Reformation,* 1957.
Man's Religions   John B. Noss. The Macmillan Company, 1962.

History of the Byzantine Empire 324–1453, Volume Two   A. A. Vasiliev.
   University of Wisconsin Press. Second English edition 1960.

Introductory Guide to the Egyptian Collections The British Museum. The Trustees of the British Museum, London, 1964.

Judaism Isidore Epstein. (Pelican) Penguin Books, Inc., 1959.

The Dead Sea Scrolls J. M. Allegro. (Pelican) Penguin Books, Inc., 1956.

The Bible As History: A Confirmation of the Book of Books Werner Keller, trs. William Neil. William Morrow & Co., Inc., 1956.

The Bible, Designed to be Read as Living Literature edited and arranged by Ernest Sutherland Bates. Simon and Schuster, Inc., 1936.

A History of the Jewish People James Parkes. Quadrangle Books, Inc., 1963.

Hinduism K. M. Sen. (Pelican) Penguin Books, Inc., 1962.

The Wonder that Was India A. L. Basham. (Paperback) Grove Press, Inc., 1959. Revised edition. Hawthorn Books, Inc.

The Concise Encyclopaedia of Living Faiths edited by R. C. Zaehner. Hawthorn Books, Inc., 1959.

The Way of Zen Alan W. Watts. Pantheon Books, Inc., 1957. (Paperback) New American Library of World Literature, Inc., 1959.

Buddhism Christmas Humphreys. (Pelican) Penguin Books, Inc., 1951.

Buddha and Buddhism Maurice Percheron. Harper & Row, Publishers, 1958.

The Path of the Buddha edited by Kenneth W. Morgan. The Ronald Press Company, 1956.

The Greeks H. D. F. Kitto. (Pelican) Penguin Books, Inc.

The Twelve Olympians Charles Seltman. (Paperback) Apollo Editions, Inc., 1962.

A History of Greek Religion   Martin P. Nilsson, trs. F. J. Fielden. Second edition. Oxford University Press, Inc. 1949. (Paperback) W. W. Norton & Company, Inc., 1964.

Five Stages of Greek Religion   Gilbert Murray. (Paperback: Anchor Books) Doubleday & Company, Inc., 1955.

The Greeks   A. W. Gomme. Oxford University Press, Inc., 1946.

The Delphic Oracle   H. W. Parke and D. E. W. Wormell, Volumes I and II. Humanities Press.

The Greeks and Their Gods   W. K. C. Guthrie. Beacon Press, 1955.

Islam in Modern History   Wilfred Cantwell Smith. Princeton University Press, 1957.

Islam   Alfred Guillaume. (Pelican) Penguin Books, Inc. Barnes & Noble, Inc., 1964.

Islam and the West   Philip K. Hitti. (Paperback) D. Van Nostrand Co., Inc., 1962.

Mohammedanism   H. A. R. Gibb. Second edition. (Paperback) Oxford University Press, Inc., 1953.

Opium of the People: The Christian Religion in the U.S.S.R.   Michael Bordeaux. Faber & Faber Ltd., London, 1965.

The Medieval Church   Ronald H. Bainton. (Paperback) D. Van Nostrand Co., Inc., 1964.

The Horizon History of Christianity   Ronald H. Bainton and the editors of Horizon Magazine. Harper & Row, Publishers, 1964.

The Pelican History of the Church   Penguin Books, Inc.

   3.   *The Reformation*   Owen Chadwick, 1964.

   4.   *The Church and the Age of Reason (1648–1789)*   G. R. Cragg. (also published by Atheneum Publishers, 1961).

   5.   *The Church in an Age of Revolution. 1789 to the Present Day*   Alec R. Vidler, 1962.

6. *A History of Christian Missions* Stephen Neill, 1964 (also published by Wm. B. Eerdmans Publishing Co., 1965).

The Social Sources of Denominationalism H. Richard Niebuhr. The Shoe String Press, Inc., 1954.

Prescott's Histories: The Rise and Decline of the Spanish Empire edited by Irwin R. Blacker. The Viking Press, Inc., 1963.

A History of Latin America Hubert Herring. Revised edition. Alfred A. Knopf, Inc., 1961.

Religion and Faith in Latin America W. Stanley Rycroft. The Westminster Press, 1958.

Index